THE HARP

Manuscript of the first page of the "Aria in Classic Style" for harp and string orchestra by Marcel Grandjany.

THE HARP

From Tara's Halls
to the
American Schools

By
ROSLYN RENSCH

PHILOSOPHICAL LIBRARY
NEW YORK

To my mother and father

CONTENTS

vii

THE HARP

CONTENTS

CHAPTER III

CHAPTER IV

CHAPTER V

CHAPTER VI

CHAPTER VII

CHAPTER VIII

SECTION III

CHAPTER I

CHAPTER II

THE HARP

CHAPTER III

CHAPTER IV

CHAPTER V

CHAPTER VI

LIST OF PLATES

xi

THE HARP

LIST OF PLATES

A BRIEF SURVEY OF THE HISTORY OF THE HARP

"Three men there are of same regard:
A king, a harper, and a bard."

FROM AN ANCIENT BRITISH
BARDIC TRIAD

SECTION I

A Brief Survey of the History of the Harp

THE HARP ranks with the drums, the cymbals, and the flute, as the oldest of man's musical instruments. Throughout the long history of the harp, the instrument has undergone numerous changes in size, shape, decoration, and construction. These factors were changed as man's musical ideas progressed, and through the ages the popularity of the harp has been comparable only to the ability of the instrument to keep pace with the musical requirements of man.

Thus, the "vicissitudes of fortune" have been many—the harp has been the most revered, and the most popular of instruments, and the most neglected. It has been revived, only to be abandoned; changed, and revived again. Yet the principle of the instrument has remained the same. The twang of the hunter's bow—so intriguing to early man—still casts its spell. The primitive bow harp is a far cry from the polished, gleaming instrument that is the modern harp; but today the ear of the twentieth century sophisticate is still wooed in the concert hall by the same process—and the harp is given life—only when man's fingers touch the strings.

CHAPTER I

The Harp In Ancient Times

IN EGYPT—Proof that the harp was an important musical instrument in the civilization of the Egyptians is evident from the extant works of art of these ancient peoples. The Egyptians possessed a variety of harps, and they depicted them in considerable detail in wall paintings and sculptures. Actual specimens of these early instruments have also been discovered in Egyptian tombs.

Probably the most remarkable of the Egyptian harp discoveries was that made in the tomb of Rameses III, at Biban-El-Moulouk, near Thebes. Two magnificent harps were found painted upon opposite walls, in one hall of the tomb. The harps, over six feet in height and elaborately decorated, were being played by white robed figures—apparently priests of a high order.

During the latter part of the 18th century, detailed sketches of these two harps were made by the English traveller James Bruce[1] (1730-1794). Numerous reproductions have been made from Bruce's sketches, and there is some difference of opinion as to the exact number of the strings on each harp. Some authorities present the smaller of the two harps as having eleven strings, while others consider thirteen to be a more accurate number. The larger harp has been credited with from twenty-one to twenty-eight strings. However, it *is* agreed that the harps found pictured in the tomb of Rameses III (which dates from about 1235 B. C.) represent the highest state of

---

[1] A letter written by Bruce and dated October 20, 1774, concerning his discovery and drawing of one of the Theban harps, is reprinted in Dr. Charles M. Burney's *A General History of Music From Earliest Ages to the Present Period* (*1789*)—1935 printing by G. T. Foulis & Company, London.

[3]

the development of the instrument in the ancient world yet to be found.

The Egyptian harp, like the harp forms of the other ancient civilizations, lacked the column, or fore-pillar, that is an important part of the harp as we know it. Though no positive information has been found revealing the type of music played on these harps, or even the scale in which they were actually tuned, it may be presumed that the absence of the column, or third side of the harp, indicates that the tension exerted on the harp frame by the strings of the largest of the Egyptian harps was not great. This leads one to believe that the strings were relatively low in pitch.

The Italian composer, Verdi, in the elaborate temple scene of his famous opera "Aida", calls for the actual appearance of Egyptian harps upon the stage. The rich chords that he has provided for the temple harps, are played on the modern harp (harps) from the opera orchestra, which has (have) been concealed backstage. The illusion created is a highly effective one.

The temple harps sketched by Bruce are representative of only one of the harp forms known to the ancient Egyptians. Besides the larger harp, these early people also had a small bow-shaped instrument, which was held in a more upright manner.

Some of the earliest examples of the Egyptian harp form date from 3,000 B. C. The harp player appearing in a wall picture with singers and flute players (found in an ancient tomb near Thebes) is designated literally as the "harp-scraper". The player is kneeling, and playing a bow-shaped harp that rests on ground level. In this position, the harp extends well over the player's left shoulder.

A later example of the Egyptian harp form has been found dating from 1300 B. C., in the time of the 20th dynasty. Like Bruce's harps, this instrument is pictured in a wall painting and is highly decorative—apparently carved and ornamented in gold. The harp is small enough to be played conveniently from a sitting position, and the musician is a woman. The shape of the harp is obviously bow-like, and as the strings are not of great length, it is reasonable to suppose that they were of a higher pitch than the strings of Bruce's harps—perhaps within the treble range. Again the harp is played "in ensemble". This time another woman, seated directly behind the harper, is clapping her hands, and a third musician is playing on a long necked banjo-type of instrument.

Another example of the Egyptian harp is to be found in a panel of street musicians, dating but a few centuries prior to the Christian era. A woman playing a tall harp of fourteen strings, leads a group of six women musicians. The instruments of the other players include: the lyre, the double flute, a banjo-like instrument, and the "shoulder-harp".[2] Several of these "shoulder harps" have been discovered in Egyptian tombs in surprising states of preservation. Musicians such as those of the above mentioned group, were probably the musical entertainers of the untitled class of the Egyptians of this period.

The Egyptian name of the harp is designated as "buni". In the Louvre, in Paris, can be found an instrument that is believed to be the oldest extant harp. It was discovered in a well-preserved condition in an Egyptian tomb. This harp apparently had twenty-one strings, and the instrument is (tri)angular in shape, rather than bow-like. It is considered to have belonged to a civilization of at least 3,500 years ago. Though the angular form of this harp differs from the curved form of the Egyptian harps depicted in the frescoes and intaglios, this harp is typical in that it also lacks a column, or fore-pillar.

The rather limited development of the harp in the several thousand years that it was known to the ancient Egyptians, apparently can be attributed to the basic precepts of the Egyp-

---

[2] The "shoulder harp" or "nanga" had a boat-shaped sound chest. The sounding-board of the instrument was of skin or parchment. The strings were fastened to a strip of wood at one end of the sound-chest, and were wound around pegs at the opposite and more bow-like extremity of the instrument. In performance, the "nanga" was held on the player's shoulder.

tian civilization. Plato, in his *Laws,* tells us that the ancient Egyptians were adverse to innovations: "To this day no alteration is allowed in these arts nor in music at all. And you will find that their works of art are painted or modeled in the same forms that they were 10,000 years ago."

A charming example of the large and small Egyptian harps as they might have looked in the time of Cleopatra, is depicted in very effective color, in the recent English motion picture version of George Bernard Shaw's "Caesar and Cleopatra".

IN BABYLON AND ASSYRIA—The music of the Babylonians was apparently evolved from that of the Sumerian civilization of Mesopotamia, and much of this Babylonian culture was then appropriated by the Assyrians. A form of harp was known to both the ancient peoples of Assyria and Babylon. A seated musician playing upon a harp of eleven strings is represented in a Babylonian sculptured tablet, which dates from 2,500 B. C.

Pictorial evidence of the Assyrian harp is to be found in the bas-reliefs excavated from mounds near the town of Mosul, in Asiatic Turkey. Here the Assyrian instrument appears to be about four feet in height. Like the harp of the ancient Egyptians, the Assyrian harp had no column. However, unlike the Egyptian harps, the Assyrian instrument was held with the sounding-body uppermost.

The Assyrian harp was apparently not a heavy instrument, for it is frequently depicted in the hands of people who seem to be dancing. While the Egyptian harp was strung with gut strings, the strings used on the Assyrian harps were of silk. The latter material is still used by the Burmese, for their harp strings.

A large group of Assyrian musicians depicted in one of the decorative reliefs which dates from 650 B. C., includes several harps. This bas-relief was discovered in the ruins of the palace of Sennacherib, king of Assyria. The leader of the musical group, two other men and four women, are all playing on harps. The instruments of the other musicians include: a form of dulcimer, the double-pipe, and a small drum. The entire group is followed closely by a chorus of women and children. This relief is now in the British museum.

IN ISRAEL—The names of the musical instruments of the ancient Hebrews are familiar to us from the many references to be found in the Bible. Since the harp was a well-known instrument to both the Egyptian and the Assyrian peoples, it is quite probable that it was also an instrument common to the ancient Hebrews. No specimens or drawings of Hebrew harps have been found, so one can only assume that their instruments were of a form similar to those of the ancient Egyptians and the Assyrians. There is also considerable speculation as to which of the Biblical names of the stringed instruments really designates the harp form.

In the first book of the Bible, Jubal is designated as the "father of all such as handle the harp". The musical instrument played by king David and called the "kinnor", may have been a small triangular harp, or some form of the lyre. The lyre was universally known among the ancient Eastern nations, and undoubtedly it preceded the other stringed instruments in antiquity.

IN ANCIENT GREECE—There is considerable evidence that the people of ancient Greece derived most of their stringed instruments from Asia. The Greeks had a form of the harp which they called "kinyra", but apparently this instrument never achieved great popularity. The numerous representations of the lyre, in the extant Greek works of art, would indicate that this instrument, rather than the harp, was their preference from among the stringed group.

The design on a Grecian vase, now in the Munich museum, provides us with the only indication of the appearance of the harp form known to the ancient Greeks. The nine muses are represented on this vase, which dates from the time of Alexander the Great. While Calliope, muse of epic poetry, and

Erato, muse of love poetry, are depicted with lyres, Polyhymnia, the muse of sacred poetry, plays the harp. Polyhymnia's harp is very similar to the harp of the ancient Assyrian peoples. It has fourteen strings, and the sounding-board portion of the harp is held uppermost, as with the Assyrian harp. (This instrument has also been identified as a psaltery.)[3]

Homer, in the ninth book of the *Iliad,* provides a reference that surely indicates that the harp of the ancient Egyptians was not unknown to the early Grecians:

"The well-wrought harp from conquered Thebes came,
Of polished silver was its costly frame."

---

[3] Webster's Dictionary identifies the psaltery as an instrument like the zither. Bede (672-735 A. D.) contrasts the psaltery to the harp in the following manner: "the harp had in its lower part the hollow portion which the psaltery had above." (From *The Story of British Music*—F. J. Crowest, see Bibliography, Section I, Chapter X.)

1

2

1. Limestone statuettes from the tomb of Nanupkau. Three harp players and a drummer; probably from Gizah, and of the 5th or 6th Egyptian dynasty.

Courtesy of the Oriental Institute University of Chicago.

2. Harper from Iraq—clay plaque from Ischali. Dated to the Isin-Larsa period, ca. 2025-1764 B.C.

Courtesy of the Oriental Institute University of Chicago.

PLATE I

2

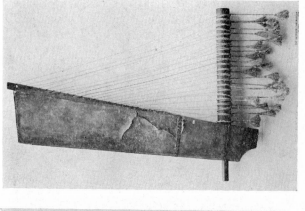

1(b)

1(a)

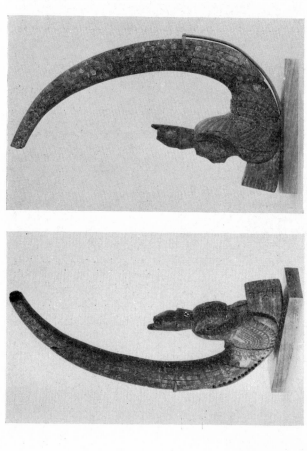

1. Model wooden harp from Egypt, dated to the 18th dynasty, ca. 1580 B.C., or later.
   (a) View of right side—note the six string holes along the lower right side of the instrument.
   (b) View of left side of harp.

   Courtesy of the Oriental Institute
   University of Chicago

2. Most ancient extant harp—the "trigone"—reproduced from original in the Louvre, Paris. The harp, dated from 1500 B.C., has 21 strings of gut. Dimensions of harp: height of sound-box—3 feet 5½ inches; length of longest string—3 feet 3½ inches; length of bar—1 foot 8 inches.

   Courtesy of the Metropolitan Museum of Art.

PLATE II

[10]

1

2

1. Wall painting of musicians at a banquet, from the tomb of Amenemhet at Sheikh Abd El Kurna, Egypt, 1475-1448 B.C. The "female singer Baket" is seated playing the harp and singing; other musicians are: a lute-player and a second woman, who plays the double pipes.

     From Nina M. Davies, *Ancient Egyptian Paintings,* plate XVII.

2. Wall painting from tomb of Zesberkera'Sonb, in the reign of Thutmose IV, 1420-1411 B.C. This female orchestra which is part of a banquet scene, includes: harp player (note that lower part of harp is covered with leopard skin) ; lute-player; dancing child; double pipe player; lyre player.

     From Nina M. Davies, *Ancient Egyptian Paintings,* plate XXXVII.

PLATE III

[11]

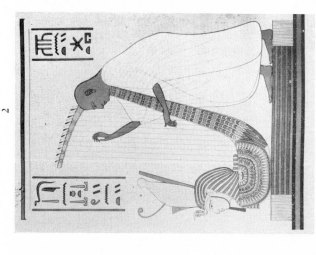

2

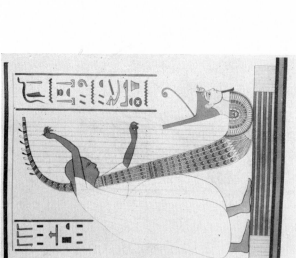

1

"Bruce's Harpers"—wall paintings from tomb of Rameses III, Biban-El-Muluk, 20th dynasty, 1235 B.C. Refrain of the harper's song reads: Receive the blessed King Rameses.

1. Harp with red crown of lower Egypt.   2. Harp with double crown of upper and lower Egypt.

From Roselli, *Monumenti Civili* (*Il Monumenti dell'Egitto* Tomo II, Pisa, 1834), plate XCVII.

PLATE IV

[12]

1

2

Assyrian harpers are depicted in wall reliefs from the Palace of Assurbanipal, Kuyunjik (Ruins of Nineveh); 8th and 7th centuries B.C.
    1. From a relief of the king and queen dining.
Courtesy of the British Museum.

    2. Harp player, lyre player, two double pipe players.
Courtesy of the Metropolitan Museum of Art.

PLATE V

[13]

1. Sutton Hoo Musical Instrument—a *provisional* reconstruction; about 11½ inches in height. Original fragments, wrapped in a beaver skin bag and preserved in a bronze bowl, include: peg-arm of maple wood; pegs of willow or poplar; main frame of maple, with mortice joint at either end; small sized tenon; fragments of oak; very thin maple sheeting.
   Courtesy of R.L.S. Bruce Mitford, assistant keeper, Dept. British & Medieval Antiquities, British Museum.

2. "Brian Boru" harp. Said to have belonged to the famous Irish monarch, Brian Boruhuha (Boiroimhe) who came to the throne in 1001 A.D. Reproduced from original in Trinity College Museum, Dublin. The harp is 3 feet 2 inches in height; and has been strung with 30 wire strings.
   Courtesy of the Metropolitan Museum of Art.

PLATE VI

CHAPTER II

The Harp In Europe

THE GREAT DIFFERENCE between the harp as it was known in
Europe during the middle ages, and the harps of the ancient
Eastern civilizations, is the fact that the European harp was
constructed of three distinct parts (or sides). To the sounding-body and the neck—often referred to as the harmonic
curve—was added the column, or fore-pillar. This column,
either straight or curving slightly outward, connected the neck
of the instrument with the sounding-body.

It is variously stated that the column was contributed to the
harp by the Celts or the Anglo-Saxons, some time before the
ninth century. If this is true, the three-sided harp may have
been the practical evolution of the angular harp of the ancient Eastern civilizations, which instrument somehow found
its way to Europe in very early times. It is also possible that
the hardy Vikings, who plundered the coast of Europe in the
eighth century, brought with them a triangular harp of their
own origin or development. In any case, the "true" harp
form, once evidenced in Europe, soon supplanted both the
curved lyre, and the quadrangular instrument which has often
been confused with the "true" harp form.

REPRESENTATIONS OF EARLY HARPS—The sculptured musician on a granite cross which stands in the churchyard of Ullard, county Kilkenny (Ireland), and is dated from the ninth
century A. D., has been the source of some confusion in the
last one hundred years. This figure, appearing on the left arm
of the cross, represents king David playing a quadrangular
musical instrument.

In 1840, Edward Bunting, Irish music antiquarian, having procured a drawing of this sculptured figure, identified the musical instrument as a harp which was lacking the column common to the other early representations of the harp in Europe. Thus, the Ullard cross figure became known as the first actual European example of the column-less harp of the ancient Eastern peoples. However, the odd proportions of this so-called harp required further investigation.

In *Old English Instruments of Music* (pages 287-288) Francis W. Galpin offers sufficient proof that king David's quadrangular musical instrument is not a column-less harp. Inspection of the actual carvings, photographs and rubbings, has revealed the presence of a column, eight inches in length, which connects the top and bottom sides of the quadrangular form. Galpin has identified the instrument as a further example of the musical instrument known as the large "cruit". This instrument, with the sounding-board placed *behind* the strings, was common to the Irish bards of the 7th to the 11th centuries. More recent discoveries, in particular, that of the Sutton Hoo musical instrument,[4] have advanced the theory that the Ullard Cross quadrangular instrument was more truly harp-like in form—actually having the sounding-board as a fourth side.

Among the earliest representations of the triangular harp form, is that to be found in an Anglo-Saxon manuscript (now in the British museum) which dates from the tenth or the eleventh century. Here king David is depicted with a small triangular harp that rests on his knees. The instrument is held by one hand and played by the other.

---

[4] A report of the lecture presented by R. L. S. Bruce Mitford, on the "Sutton Hoo Musical Instrument" can be found in the *British Archaeological News Letter* (see Bibliography). This Saxon instrument is dated from the 7th century. It is interesting to note that maple wood, which is used in the present-day concert harp, was also utilized in fashioning this early harp form. The Sutton Hoo musical instrument was found in the richest of all Saxon graves. While other objects in the grave were of Byzantine, Swedish, Frankish or native British origin, the birds' head escutcheons on this instrument have definitely identified it as of Saxon craftsmanship.

A bas-relief from the abbey of St. Georges de Bocherville, now in the museum of Rouen, depicts a further example of the eleventh century harp. In this relief eleven musicians and a tumbler are represented. Counting from the left, the seventh and the tenth minstrels in the group are playing on harp forms. Both of these harpers are wearing crowns. The seventh minstrel plays on a small species of harp that is definitely triangular in form. The sounding-board of this instrument, however, is placed behind the strings, as with the previously mentioned "cruit". The harp of the tenth musician is more in keeping with our concepts of the instrument. The harper is trying the strings with the fingers of his left hand, while with his right hand he appears to be manipulating a large tuning key.

THE IRISH HARP AND THE "CYTHARA ANGLICA"—A drawing of a triangular twenty-three string harp was found on a relic case, dated 1350, which contained the tooth of St. Patrick. And it has been established that in Ireland, as early as 1251 A. D., the Irish harp was placed on the coat of arms of the king; painted on the public buildings; and stamped on the coins. Dante gives as the reason for this constant use of the harp, the fact that the peoples of that island believed themselves to be descendants of the prophet David.

While the harp is closely allied with the early Irish peoples, the triangular twelve stringed harp that is represented in a manuscript found in the monastery of St. Blaise, is clearly identified as "Cythara anglica". (The manuscript itself has been variously dated as a product of the ninth, or of the twelfth or thirteenth centuries.)

To strengthen further the cause of the historians who believe that the Celts (more specifically the Irish) borrowed the triangular harp form from the "anglica", rather than originated it themselves, can be added the words of Venantius Fortunatus, the Bishop of Poictiers. Writing during the early part of the seventh century, the Bishop states: "Let the Barbarian sing to the harp". The name "Barbarian" could hardly be applied to the advanced Christian civilization of the Irish, but such a term could conceivably refer to the invading Angles, Saxons and Northmen.

However, Diodorus Siculus, the Greek historian, who lived in the first century B. C., tells of an island "the size of Sicily", where most of the inhabitants of a city consecrated to Apollo played on harps (also translated as "instruments like lyres") while chanting hymns in the temple. The island that Diodorus thus describes has been identified by Flood, in *The Story of the Harp* and *The History of Irish Music,* as Ireland. And the theory has been advanced that the harp was brought to Ireland by the Phoenicians in 1300 B. C.[5]

Whether the triangular harp form can be attributed to the ancestors of the Irish, the English, or the Scandinavian peoples, remains the unanswered question. However, there is sufficient evidence to prove that the harp was a favorite instrument of the Anglo-Saxons, the German and Celtic bards, and the Scandinavian Scalds.

THE NORTHMEN—References to the harp can be found in the great Sagas of the Vikings or Northmen. These Sagas were perpetuated by the Scandinavian Scalds, and poetry or Scaldship, was considered to be a gift from the gods. The Scalds were welcomed wherever they journeyed, and their talents were often richly rewarded.

The harp was included in the orchestra of the Viking king Hugleik, and regular performers were kept by a number of chiefs. While no description of the size or shape of the Viking harps can be found, it may be presumed that at least one type of harp was very large. For it is recorded that as a little girl, Aslaug, wife of Ragner Lodbrok, could be hidden in a harp.

---

[5] A prospectus, concerning a book to be written by John Gunn on the early history of the harp, was included in Gunn's *An Historical Enquiry* (see Bibliography) published in 1801. In this future book, Gunn intended to trace the origin of the European harp from Pegu, in Burma. Other theories have been advanced which concern the travels of the Aryans.

The Sagas of Herraud and Bosi further state that a man could stand upright in a harp. This does not seem too incredible when one considers that the ancient Romans were known to have built lyres as big as sedan chairs.

The intricate wood carvings of the Vikings give us our only examples of the harps of those peoples. The portal of Opdal church in Numedal, Norway, presents a detailed picture of one Gunnar in the snake-pit, and also includes a representation of Gunnar's harp. The triangular instrument, which lies at his feet, has nine or ten strings, and the harp appears to be more than one third as tall as the carved figure of the man. Gunnar is listed as a very skilled harper; so skilled in fact, that on the carved door-jambs of Hyllestan church (Soetersdal), Gunnar, still in the snake-pit with his hands tied behind his back, is pictured as playing the harp with his toes! This harp, however, does not seem to be of the same proportions as the harp in the preceding carving. The latter instrument, viewed from the front, is more in the form of a figure "eight".

In England, Scotland and Wales—The legend of Alfred the Great entering the Danish camp (878 A. D.) disguised as a harper, gives us some indication of the prominence of the harp among the Anglo-Saxons in the ninth and tenth centuries. These peoples referred to the harp as "hearpe", derived from the Anglo-Saxon word "to pluck".

The Welsh bards were early connected with the Irish bards, and it is possible that the early Welsh minstrelsy was somewhat derived from that of the Irish. However, it is also possible that the people of Wales developed the harp from the Greek specimen; and the musical and poetical contests at the Eisteddfoudau—known from time immemorial in Wales—have been likened to the Olympic games of the ancient Greeks.

The Welsh called their harp "telyn", possibly from the buzzing sound produced by the hair strings. The ability to play the harp was required of all Welsh gentlemen, and the Welsh laws designated three lawful harps: (1) the harp of the king; (2) the harp of the master of music; and (3) the harp of a gentleman. The harp could not be touched by a slave, and the instrument was exempt from seizure for debts.

The Scots strung their harps with strings of wire, or of gut, and they referred to the harp as the "clarsach". The drastic enactments against the Scottish bards, by Macbeth, in the eleventh century, did much to curtail the activities of the harpers in Scotland.

IN IRELAND—It was a tradition, at the gatherings of the early Irish Parliament, to follow the day's business with minstrelsy in the banquet hall. The Parliament, or Feis, met periodically at Tara, in the county of Mearth, until the gathering was cursed by St. Ruadhan, in 560 A. D. The harp was ever after silent in Tara's halls, but the incident has been immortalized in song.

From the sixth to the ninth centuries, there are numerous references to the harp in Irish literature. Various annals list the deaths of important harpers and mention the extensive use of the harp on special occasions. Two of the nine musical instruments mentioned as being in general use among the ancient Irish (in the manuscripts of the Irish monks of St. Gall, dating from 650 to 900 A. D.) are considered to be members of the harp family—the "cruit" (previously mentioned in this chapter) and the "clairseach". Flood designates the "cruit" as a small harp or lyre, while the "clairseach" was a larger instrument, used for festive occasions.

DANTE ON THE IRISH HARP—The Irish harp was a well-known instrument in Europe. Dante, writing in the thirteenth century, praises the construction of the Irish harps and the remarkable ability of the harpers. He states that the Irish harp was considerably larger than the Italian harp, and it was strung with strings of brass and steel wire. Quite unlike the present way of playing the harp, the Irish method required that the harper have *long* finger-nails with which to pluck the strings.

As changes occurred in the harmonic system, the stringing and tuning of the harp was probably altered accordingly. The addition of more strings to the harp brought about a change in the appearance of the instrument. Two of the three sides of the harp—the column and the sounding-body—were made longer; while the neck, or harmonic curve, of the instrument remained the same. This adjustment produced a taller harp, of more slender proportions. The minstrel's harp of the fifteenth century was of this form.

ENACTMENTS AGAINST THE HARPERS—By 1402, the Welsh minstrels were so active in resistance movements against the British that an enactment was passed which forbade the Welsh to retain minstrels. And by 1563, the harp was an instrument of such national significance in Ireland that Queen Elizabeth decreed that all Irish harpers were to be hung! This prompted a large number of the minstrels to leave Ireland for the continent, where they were eagerly received.

GALILEO ON THE HARP—Vincent di Galileo (father of the philosopher and mathematician) wrote during the sixteenth century (Dialogo della Musica Antica e Moderna) that the Irish double harps—having two rows of strings—were common in Italy. The Italian harps used in the early opera orchestras were much the same as the Irish instruments.

Throughout the Renaissance the sweet-toned harp was second only to the lute, in favor among the instruments of the plucked-string group. This harp was a larger instrument than its predecessor. The addition of still more strings had caused the neck of the harp to be lengthened, so that the three separate parts of the harp were again more equal in proportion.

EXTANT HARPS—Seven specimens of the harp as it was known in the British Isles before the eighteenth century are extant. Three of these harps were perhaps made prior to the sixteenth century. Two of these harps are considered to be Scottish instruments—the queen Mary harp, said to have belonged to Mary queen of Scots prior to 1563; and the Lamont harp. There is some question as to whether this latter instrument was of Scottish or of Irish origin. It is said to have belonged to a harper who died in Scotland around 1650.[6]

THE BRIAN BORU HARP—The oldest of these early harps is probably the best known—the Brian Boru or O'Brian harp. The fabulous legend concerning this harp lists it as the instrument of Brian Boruhuha (Boiroimhe), an Irish monarch of the eleventh century.

The Brian Boru harp originally had one set of thirty strings. The strings were of wire, attached to brass tuning-pins. The instrument measures thirty-two inches in height; the column is of oak, and the sounding-board of red sallow. The extreme end of the neck (equivalent to the crown of the modern harp) is partly capped with hand-wrought silver, and contains a large crystal set in silver, and the setting for another stone. The string holes in the sounding-board of the harp are ornamented with escutcheons of brass. The base of the harp is broken and the wood has decayed, however, it is quite evident that this harp is the work of a highly skilled craftsman. The O'Brian, or Brian Boru, harp is now housed in Trinity College, Dublin.[7]

---

[6] An interesting version of the family history of the Lamont Harp can be found in *An Historical Enquiry* by John Gunn. (See Bibliography). In 1904 the Queen Mary harp was purchased at auction by the Edinburgh Antiquarian Museum.

[7] The most complete information on the aforementioned harps can be found in Robert Bruce Armstrong's detailed and beautifully illustrated book, *The Irish and the Highland Harps* (see Bibliography). Although only 180 copies of this book were printed (in 1904), American libraries have been fortunate in securing editions. Mention is also made, in this volume, of missing specimens of Irish and Highland harps, and those known to have been destroyed or lost.

THE HARP IN EUROPE

"Oh minstrel harp still must thine accents sleep?
. . . .
Not thus in ancient days of Caledon
Was thy voice mute amid the festal crowd,
When lay of hopeless love, or glory won,
Amused the fearful, or subdued the proud."

SCOTT, *Lady of the Lake*

A representation of King David with the harp heads this illuminated first page, from a late 13th century Psalter, now in the British Museum.

From Henry Shaw, *Art of Illumination,* Bell & Daldy, London, 1870.

PLATE VII

25

"Madonna and Child with Angels" oil painting by Master of Fucecchio (Italian Florentine School active first part of 15th century). The angels seated on either side of the Madonna, are playing on minstrel's harps.

Photograph by H. Brammer; Courtesy of the Nicholas M. Acquavella Galleries, New York City.

PLATE VIII

CHAPTER III

Prelude to the Pedal Harp

THE HARP, as it has already been noted, was included in the groups of musical instruments used to accompany the early Italian operas. In Paris in 1581, harps were used in the instrumental ensemble which accompanied Balthasarini's "Ballet Comique de la Reine". The "orchestra" for this lavish production included: oboes, flutes, cornets, trombones, violas di gamba, lutes, bassoon, and ten violins, as well as the harps. The musicians, however, did not play together but were separated into ten bands. Each band was to accompany some particular character, or set of characters, in the ballet. The harps were combined with the flutes, for king Neptune and his followers.

In Florence in 1589, the early Italian composers, Cavaliere, Marenzio and Caccini, combining their talents for entre' acte music (for presentation during the marriage festivities of the Grand Duke Ferdinand) used harps, with lyres, viols and lutes. One of the playlets given on this occasion concerned the adventures of the mythical Arion, and a vocal solo with harp accompaniment was featured. The orchestral pioneer, Monteverdi, called for the use of the double harp, in the score of his opera "Orfeo", produced in 1608 in Mantua, Italy.

BACON'S "BROKEN MUSICK" ESSAY—Sir Francis Bacon, in his essay on "Broken Musick or Concert Musick" ("Broken Musick" refers to the combinations of instruments of different families) states: "Some concerts of instruments are sweeter than others; as the Irish harp, and the bass viall agree well; the recorder and stringed musick; organs and voice, etc. But

[27]

virginalls and pipes; or Welsh harp and Irish harp; or voice and pipes alone, agree not so well."

It is from such information that we know that the harp was used in ensemble playing during the sixteenth and the seventeenth centuries in Europe. However, the harp was principally a diatonic instrument. As such, it was incapable of producing the chromatic alterations required by the type of music developing in Europe at this time. A re-tuning, or the shortening of a harp string by pressure of the finger, could produce a desired chromatic alteration. However, either of these processes would cause an undesired interruption in the flow of harp music.

THE DOUBLE HARP—The double harp previously mentioned in this history, has been designated as the harp with two rows of strings. Two different methods of tuning the double harp have been advanced. It is quite possible that both of these methods were used at various times:

(1) The two rows of strings were tuned in unison, in the desired mode or scale. Thus, a separate row of strings was provided for each hand and the volume of tone produced was greater.

(2) (As suggested in John Thomas' *History of the Harp*) The row of strings on the right side of the harp was tuned diatonically from top string (highest) to center string; the continuation of this row was then tuned to the accidentals. The row of strings on the left side of the harp was tuned in the opposite manner—accidentals from the top to center and the diatonic scale from center to the lowest string. Since the right hand was used to play in the treble, and the left hand, the bass, it was only necessary to put the fingers through to the strings of the opposite side, to produce the required accidental. The "only" however, is a rather large one, for the inconvenience of this procedure, especially in fast passages, can well be imagined. Neither this development of the double

harp, or the following evolution, solved the problem of rapid modulation on the harp.

THE WELSH TRIPLE HARP—Early in the 17th century, the Welsh triple harp was developed. This harp was provided with three rows of strings. The outer rows were tuned diatonically (throughout) in unison, while the inner row of strings provided the needed accidentals. The Welsh triple harp was a tall instrument with a compass of at least four octaves; one can well imagine how cumbersome such an instrument of 97 or 98 strings would be for the harp player.

THE TYROLEAN INVENTION—A more successful solution to the problem, than that of the double harp and the triple harp, was developed in the Tyrol, in the latter part of the 17th century. Along the neck of the diatonically tuned harp, with its one row of strings, was placed a little row of pivoted hooks. The pressure of one of these hooks against the string of the harp, raised the pitch of that particular string by a semi-tone.

Early in the 18th century—more specifically at some time between 1720 and 1740—a mechanism, connecting the hooks (in octaves) along the neck of the harp, with pedals that could be operated by the feet of the player, was evolved. The proportions of the harp were naturally altered to permit this change. The foot pedals required that the harp should stand on floor level to be played (as with the Welsh triple harp); and the pedal rods, running through the column of the instrument, necessitated the complete straightening of that column.

It is really doubtful as to which of the early harp-makers can be credited with the idea of the first pedal mechanism. Madame de Genlis (harpist; and governess to the French Royal family of Louis Phillippe) mentions one Gaiffre as the inventor; the historian Fetis lists the Bavarian, Hochbrucker; Dr. Burney considers that Simon of Brussels was the inventor; Goepffert, a professor of harp, is also credited with the invention; and it is known that a resident of Nuremburg, Paul Velter, produced a pedal harp in 1730. Other possible inventors

THE HARP

include: Louvet, Salmon, Holtzmann, Lepine, Nadermann and Cousineau.

Undoubtedly the most interesting fact to be surmised from this information is that of the general interest evidenced in the problem presented by the diatonic character of the harp.

ORCHESTRAL USE OF THE HARP—The harp was not a favorite instrument with orchestral composers of the 18th and early 19th centuries. This can be well understood when one considers that the harp did not attain the basis for its present compass until 1810. All the orchestral composers prior to that date had at their disposal only the wire strung Irish double harp and the gut strung Italian double harp; the Welsh triple harp; and the later, still limited, single action harp.

Conductors and composers who have transcribed the orchestral works of the classicists for the modern orchestra, frequently have added parts for one or two harps. Solo music from the works of the classic composers has been added to the repertoire of the modern harp by transcriptions and arrangements made by present-day concert harpists.

Bach did not use the harp in any of his works. Handel first tried the harp in "Julius Caesar" in 1713. In his Oratorio, "Esther" (1720), he included parts for two Welsh harps. Handel also wrote a "Concerto in Bb" for the harp—to be played during the intermission of his opera "The Alexander Feast". This concerto, as revised by the eminent French harpist, Marcel Grandjany (see Section III—Suggested Music, Chapters IV and VI) has become an important addition to the modern concert harp repertoire.

Gluck used the harp for lyre effects in his opera "Orpheus". A number of lesser known French composers of this period also included parts for the single action harp in their operas (Mehul—"Utal" and "Joseph"; Lesueur—"Les Bardes"). Haydn did not include the harp in his orchestra, but reference is made to a "sonata" he composed for harp, flute and double bass. The Mozart "Concerto in C Major" (K299) for flute,

harp and orchestra, was composed at the insistence of the Duc de Guisnes. (The duc, himself, played the flute, and his daughter was a most promising harpist.) This work, of great piquant charm, is Mozart's sole contribution to the literature for the harp. Beethoven used the harp only once—in his ballet "The Creations of Prometheus", first produced in 1801.

Woodcut by Hans Burgkmair, "Die Geschicklichkeit in der Musik", an illustration from the novel "Der Weisskunig", written in praise of the emperor, ca. 1514-1516.

Courtesy of the Metropolitan Museum of Art.

PLATE IX

31107

2

1

1. "A Musical Soirée", oil painting by Girolamo Forni active second half of the 16th century, Venice, Italy.

Courtesy of the Metropolitan Museum of Art.

2. Gallery view of 18th century harps, Crosby Brown collection Metropolitan Museum of Art. The center instrument is a "Telyn" or Welsh harp, in Japanese style, made by John Richards of Llanrwst, Wales, in 1775. Dimensions of Welsh harp: length of front pillar—6 feet 6 inches; range of harp—five octaves; 98 strings of gut.

Courtesy of the Metropolitan Museum of Art.

[34]

PLATE X

CHAPTER IV

The Single Action Pedal Harp

HOCHBRUCKER—In 1720, Hockbrucker, a native of Dona-werth in Bavaria, made a harp with five pedals, to be operated by the feet of the harp player. These pedals were connected to crooks set along the neck, or harmonic curve, of the harp, by means of the pedal rods running through the column of the instrument. Each pedal controlled the string, for which it was named, throughout the octaves. The five pedals installed by Hochbrucker controlled the C, D, F, G and A strings. When one of these pedals was pressed down, the strings it affected were raised one semi-tone by the crook device in the neck. The great draw-back to this development was that the action of the crook pulled the strings out of line and often out of tune as well.

Hochbrucker soon advanced his pedals to seven—one for each tone of the diatonic scale (C, D, E, F, G, A and B). These harps were tuned in the key of E*b*, and eight major and five minor scales were possible on the single action harp, from this tuning.

STECHT AND MEYER—Around 1740, a German musician named Stecht is said to have introduced the pedal harp into France. Credit for this introduction is also claimed by biographers of one Phillip Meyer. This Strasburg born musician, who was self-taught as a harpist, went to Paris for music study some years prior to 1760. In Paris, Meyer's suggestions for the pedal harp were adopted by Nadermann, senior. Meyer later travelled on to London and helped popularize the pedal harp there. He was among the first to publish a Method for the pedal harp.

THE COUSINEAUS—By 1752, two Frenchmen—the Cousineaus, father and son—had improved upon Hochbrucker's pedal invention. They dispensed with the crooks, substituting two small metal plates which shortened the string by gripping it (referred to as the "Crutch" mechanism). In 1762, Prince Michael Casimir Oginski is said to have added further pedals to the harp. This distinguished amateur musician was the author of the article on the harp which appeared in the first edition of the French Encyclopedia.

In 1780, the enterprising Cousineaus doubled the pedals of the harp—making fourteen in all—and the connecting mechanism as well. The harp could then be tuned in the key of C♭, and it was possible to play in fifteen keys—if the labyrinth of pedals could be managed.

The improvements extended to the harp in continental Europe made little impression on the English and Irish peoples of the time. The classic comment on the pedal harp, written by Dr. Charles M. Burney, music historian, could also be attributed to the modern musician, apathetically interested in this instrument. Of Simon's harp, Dr. Burney stated: ". . . and the natural notes are in the diatoned scale; the rest are made by the feet; . . ." (!)

THE HARPS OF MARIE ANTOINETTE—The South Kensington Museum in England, now houses the charming and ornate French pedal harp, made by Nadermann, in 1780, for the ill-fated French queen Marie Antoinette. Like the other early pedal harps, the Nadermann instrument was equipped with hooks which pulled the string out of the plane when raising it the required semi-tone.

The George F. Harding Museum, in Chicago, owns another harp attributed to Marie Antoinette. A glass panel was inserted along the neck of this instrument, apparently so that the workings of the inner mechanism of the harp might be seen by the queen and her court. As recently as 1946, another French harp, said to have been made for Marie Antoinette (lost during the French revolution; discovered in 1830 in an attic in the Nancy town hall; and finally presented to the Academy of Music) was re-strung for use in concerts of historical musical instruments in Paris.

ERARD'S PEDAL MECHANISM—The French revolution curtailed the activities of the Cousineaus, and no significant improvement was made in the harp, until Sebastian Erard received the first English patent ever to be granted for the harp, in 1792. Erard, who was born in Strasburg in 1752, had an established reputation as a Parisian piano maker, when he fled to London during the French revolution. Investigation into the possibilities of a more adequate pedal mechanism for the harp occupied much of his time after 1786.

By 1794, Sebastian Erard had produced a single action harp of great superiority. Probably the most noticeable improvement evidenced in this harp was Erard's "forked" mechanism. The hooks, crooks, and crutches of the earlier pedal harps had been supplanted by a revolving fork mechanism. In the first experiment with this type of action, the forks were hidden behind the brass neck-plate. They moved through quarter circles cut in the plate.

The principle of the forked mechanism—a small metal disc, with the two small metal prongs protruding from opposite sides—is still utilized in the modern harp. Each harp string, running from tuning-pin (and bridge-pin) to the sounding-board, passed over the center of the disc. When the C pedal, for example, was pressed down, the mechanism in the neck of the harp (which was connected to the foot pedals by rods running through the harp column, as has previously been described) caused the small discs (placed along the neck of the harp in back of all the C strings) to revolve. The two forks, pressing against the string on opposite sides, raised the string one semi-tone—and C sharp was produced from the strings originally tuned to C natural.

Throughout the entire procedure, the harp string was not

removed from the original plane, and the sound that could be produced on the raised string was as clear as the sound produced on the open string.

There are several examples of the Sebastian Erard single action harp still to be found in this country. The popularity of the harp and the great interest evidenced in the instrument, following Erard's improvements, are well attested by the fact that so many of these harps were imported to America.

The proportions of the harp were somewhat changed by Erard. His early single action harp is characterized by its gracefully curving neck and the slender fluted column, with three carved rams' heads decorating the crown. Prior to Erard, the sounding-body of the harp had been built in staves, like that of the lute or the mandoline. Erard built the sounding-body in but two sections, generally using sycamore wood. The sounding-board was of Swiss pine. The body of the harp was strengthened on the inside by ribs. The single action harp was tuned in E♭, to permit music in the following keys—E♭, B♭, F, C, G, D, A and E.

IRISH HARP REVIVAL AND THE ROYAL PORTABLE HARP—In 1792, the same year that Erard brought out his improved single-action for the pedal harp, an attempt was made to revive the ancient harp music in Ireland. A meeting of the remaining bards was held in Belfast. It was at this gathering that Edward Bunting (1773-1843), acting as secretary, collected the ancient Irish airs, which he subsequently published, preserving them for later generations.

Robert Bruce Armstrong, in his volume *English and Irish Instruments* (see Bibliography) has devoted an entire chapter to the "Royal Portable" Irish harps of John Egan, of Dublin. The first harp made by Egan is displayed in the Crosby Brown Collection of Musical Instruments, at the Metropolitan Museum, in New York City. Egan's fourth harp, of which mention is made in Armstrong's book, is dated 1819. In appearance the Egan harp is much like the charming Irish harps made in this country, since 1913, by Melville Clark, of Syracuse, New York.

In an attempt to put the Irish harp on a competitive basis with the French pedal harp, Egan placed seven "stops"—A, E, B, F, C, G and D—on the inner side of the curved forepillar of his harp. When pressed down by the thumb, these stops acted upon the harp strings, raising them a semi-tone (by the same principle of shortening the string). Egan's harps were strung with gut strings rather than the wire strings of the earlier Irish harps. The instruments were painted blue, green or black, and were decorated with the traditional Irish shamrocks.

The Royal Portable harp enjoyed some vogue in the British Isle, and was copied by other harp-makers. The greater compass of the pedal harp, however, soon gave this instrument precedence over the Irish harp. Further attempts to revive the art of playing the Irish harp were also unsuccessful at this time.

Italian psaltery and cover, 18th century. A musical group, including a man playing a portable harp with music stand attached, decorates the inside of the psaltery cover.

Courtesy of the
Metropolitan Museum of Art.

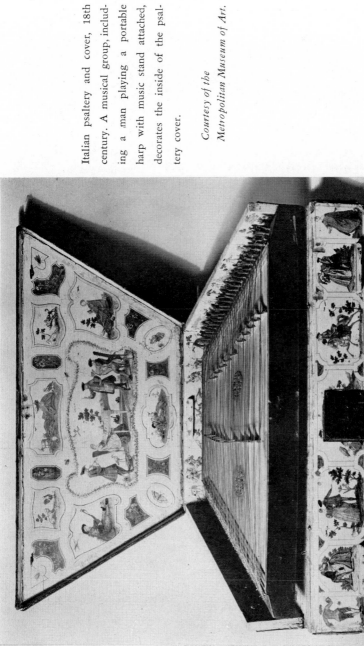

PLATE XI

[41]

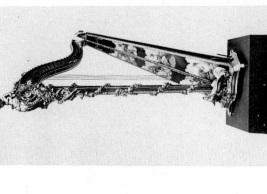

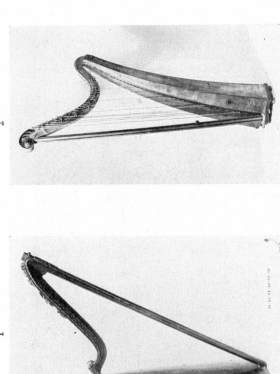

1. Harp said to have belonged to Charles II of England, about 1670. The carving—faces, masks, etc.—was done by Grinling Gibbons. Dimensions: length of front pillar—6 feet 3½ inches; length of body—4 feet 5 inches. In general appearance, the harp resembles the triple string Welsh harp (note string holes in sounding-board) of the 17th and 18th centuries.

By Courtesy of the Victoria and Albert Museum.

2. Hooked harp, Germany early 18th century. Inscribed "Martin Eggert in Wettingen". Length of front pillar—5 feet 4 inches. The harp has 36 strings of gut, and it is equipped with nine large brass hooks (see harmonic curve) that can be turned to raise the pitch of the harp string.

Courtesy of the Metropolitan Museum of Art.

3. French harp, period of Louis XVI, said to have belonged to Queen Marie Antoinette. Dimensions: height—5 feet 5 inches; width—2 feet 8 inches. The column, carved and gilded, in style of Vernis Martin with painted wreaths of flowers and musical instruments; at the foot are two cocks. The harp is a single action pedal harp.

By Courtesy of the Victoria and Albert Museum.

PLATE XII

[42]

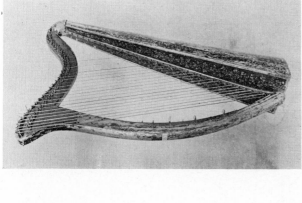

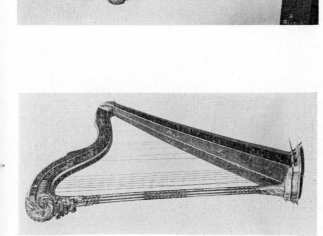

1. Single action French pedal harp, dating from the second half of the 18th century. The harp is lacquered and painted with scenes after the Chinese. Note the staved body.

   Courtesy of the Metropolitan Museum of Art.

2. Single action pedal harp of late 18th century, made by Nadermann of Paris. The instrument is painted blue; Corinthian style pillar—5 feet 7 inches in height. The body is formed of seven strips of wood; there are seven pedals; 42 strings.

   Courtesy of the Metropolitan Museum of Art.

3. Egan Portable Harp, dated 1319. Dimensions: 3 feet 1 inch in height; 34 gut strings. The disc mechanism (similar to Erard's) can be seen on the harmonic curve—this mechanism is controlled by seven small levers (ditals) on the inner curve of the column.

   Courtesy of the Metropolitan Museum of Art.

PLATE XIII

An early 19th century illustration from Bochsa's *Standard Tutor for the Harp* published by Edwin Ashdown, London. The harp column is of the Grecian style. Note the position of the hands on the harp strings.

PLATE XIV

[44]

CHAPTER V

The Double Action Pedal Harp

SEBASTIAN ERARD'S DOUBLE ACTION—From 1801 to 1809, Sebastian Erard worked on the pedal mechanism of his harp, to further the possibilities of modulation. In June of the year 1810, he secured a patent on his "double action" development for the harp. As explained in the chapter on Pedals (Section II—Fundamentals) in this book, Erard, with only seven pedals, was able to achieve the results that the Cousineaus had attempted with fourteen pedals. The harp could now be tuned in the key of C flat, and readily played in the keys of: G♭, D♭, A♭, E♭, B♭, F, C, G, D, A, E, B, F♯, and C♯—fifteen major and twelve minor scales in all.

The double action harp possessed twenty-one sounds in the octave, as compared to twelve for the keyboard instruments. Modulation to all keys was possible; the fingering for all keys remained the same; and the "double action" of the pedals produced the enharmonic tones, upon which the characteristic harp glissando is based.

Sebastian Erard died in Paris in 1831. His nephew, Pierre, carried on the business until his death in 1855. The Grecian harp column, characteristic of Sebastian Erard's double action harp, was superseded by the Gothic column, patented by Pierre Erard in 1836. Many examples of these two types of harp column can be found among the European harps in this country.

The Gothic column Erard harp was a larger and more powerful instrument than its predecessor. Pierre Erard's harp was distinguished by the greater distance between the strings, and the broadened sounding-board. A fine example of this Erard Gothic harp, in the style of Louis XVI, is now owned by Alberto Salvi, the concert artist. This exquisite harp is said to have belonged to the Emperor Franz Joseph of Austria.

MR. PIGOT'S HARP—Here, perhaps, the author may be permitted to digress from the chronological history of the harp, to relate a personal experience concerning one of the Erard harps imported to America. This charming instrument, a double action harp, of light maple wood (including a column and crown of polished maple) decorated with flower designs and a Chinese pagoda, was discovered in a shop on Chicago's Clark Street. A search of the early records kept by Erard of London, disclosed that this harp was first sold in 1839, to a Mr. Pigot of Dublin, Ireland.

Reference is made to the Pigot family of Dublin, in P. W. Joyce's *Old Irish Folk Music*—published by Longman, Green & Company, of London, 1909. A part of the collection of Irish airs included in this book, were assembled between 1840 and 1850 by a John Edward Pigot, Dublin barrister and Hon. Secretary of the "Society for the Preservation and Publication of the Melodies of Ireland" (founded in Dublin, 1851). One cannot but wonder if this gentleman, who evidenced such an interest in Irish music, was not also the first owner of this quaint harp. Portions of the wood of this more than 100-year old instrument have been eaten away. This condition can also be noted in the extant specimens of the early Irish harp.

EXTENDED USE OF THE HARP—The addition of pedals to the harp, and the subsequent improvement of the double action, provided a much needed stimulus for the harp. In its new form, the instrument set out to conquer new fields. Young ladies had already discovered that the harp provided an excellent opportunity to display "pretty hands, well rounded arms and a neat foot". Now the greater compass of the harp provided a fitting vehicle for the serious virtuoso, and the harp could be added to the concert orchestra without apology.

Louis Spohr, German violinist and composer, whose first wife, Dorette Scheidler, was a fine harpist, composed a number of chamber works for the harp at this time.

In France, the composer François Boieldieu, was the first to utilize the harmonics of the harp in an orchestral score. His opera "La Dame Blanche", first presented in 1825, successfully combined the harp with oboe, French horns, bassoon and strings. Meyerbeer included parts for two harps in several of his operas—"Robert le Diable" (1831), "The Prophet", etc.

Berlioz not only used the harp in his orchestral scores, but his comprehensive treatment of the problem of writing for the harp—as set down in his *Treatise* (see Bibliography)—served as a guide for many later composers. Berlioz contended that the effectiveness of the harp, in orchestral use, was in proportion to the number of harps used. In his "Faust" he called for ten harps.

EVOLUTION OF SCHOOLS OF HARP PLAYING—The evolution of the Parisian, the Viennese, the London, and the Berlin schools of harp playing, has all been traced back to the same source: The father of the Austrian-born composer, Franz Joseph Haydn, was a wheelwright. On Sunday, after morning church services, the principal amusement in the simple home of the Haydn family was the singing of Haydn's mother, accompanied on the harp by the composer's father.

The elder Haydn, who was self-taught on the harp—as were many music-loving German artisans of his time—taught the young Johan Baptist Krumpholz to play the harp. This Hungarian musician was a friend of both the younger Haydn, and also of Beethoven. Krumpholz became a talented harpist, as well as a composer for the instrument, and harp-maker.[8] He taught Nadermann, who subsequently instructed Bochsa and Felix Godefroid, in Paris. Bochsa taught Francis Dizi[9] and Elias Parish-Alvars. The latter harpist was the teacher of

---

[8] Krumpholz, with the assistance of Nadermann senior, is credited with extending the compass of the harp, and adding the swell pedal to the instrument.

[9] Dizi, who achieved particular fame for the beauty of his tone, invented the so-called perpendicular harp, and effected other improvements—as the substitution of a damper pedal for the swell pedal. These improvements were later found impractical and were discontinued.

THE HARP

Gottlieb Kruger, who in turn taught Alphonse Hasselmans. Hasselmans' pupils included: Marcel Tournier, Henriette Renie, Margaret Achard (Prothin), Ada Sassoli, Lily Laskine, Gertrude Ina Robinson, Cecilia Praetorius, and Raphael Martenot.

The harp classes at the Paris Conservatoire were founded in 1825. François Joseph Nadermann (son of the harp-maker) was the first professor of harp. Antoine Prumier followed Nadermann as instructor, teaching from 1835 to 1867. Prumier was succeeded by Theodore Labarre; and in 1870, Labarre was succeeded by Ange Conrad Prumier, the son of Antoine. It is said that the Prumiers continued the peculiar method of playing the harp with all five fingers—a system also attributed to Madame de Genlis.

Alphonse Hasselmans followed A. C. Prumier as professor of harp at the Paris Conservatoire, in 1884. A number of the finest harpists now concertizing, teaching and composing in America, received their training from Hasselmans and his famous pupils.

Returning to the Viennese school of harp playing, we find that Parish-Alvars (pupil of Bochsa) taught Zamara, senior, who in turn instructed his son. The younger Zamara was the teacher of the Schuecker brothers—Edmund and Heinrich, F. Moser, Alfred Holy, the Mosshammer brothers, Alfred Kastner and Cecilia Praetorius. A number of these fine artists later came to America to live.

The Berlin school of harp playing is traced from Parish-Alvars to Charles Oberthur and Carl Constantin Grimm. Grimm instructed Albert Zabel and Wilhelm Posse; and Posse taught Alex Slepoushkin, who traveled not to America, but to Russia.

The London school follows from the above mentioned Bochsa, first harp instructor at the Royal Academy of Music in London. Bochsa instructed the Chattertons; John Balsir Chatterton was the teacher of John Thomas. Thomas numbered Butler and the younger Cockerill among his pupils. T. H. Wright, another prominent English harpist of Thomas' time, had in 1819, as a very young child, received instruction from Nadermann.

TWO EARLY VIRTUOSI—The years from 1820-1845 were extremely brilliant ones for the harp in Europe. Parish-Alvars, Bochsa, Dizi, Theodore Labarre, Leon Gatayes, Xavier Desargues and the Godefroid brothers, Felix and Jules, all achieved great prominence as virtuoso musicians during this period. The brief nature of this history does not permit a complete listing of all the important harp players, nor does it permit the inclusion of biographical material on even the aforementioned harpists. However, the two best-known of the early virtuosi cannot be overlooked—Robert Nicholas Charles Bochsa and Elias Parish-Alvars.

Bochsa was born in France, of Bohemian parents, in 1789. His earliest musical endeavors were concerned with the study of the flute and composition. In 1806, the young Bochsa commenced the serious study of the harp, receiving instruction from Nadermann and Marie Martin Martel, the vicomte de Marin. Bochsa's proficiency on the harp brought the appointment of harpist to Napoleon Bonaparte, in 1813. Following the restoration of Louis XVIII to the French throne, Bochsa was appointed royal harpist in 1816. In his years as a court musician, Bochsa continually astonished his listeners by the new effects he was able to produce on the harp, and by his orchestral ability.

In 1817, however, Bochsa was obliged to leave France to escape being jailed for forgery. He turned to friends in London. At the same time that the harpist was being tried in absentia, convicted and heavily fined, in the Parisian courts, he was commencing a highly successful career with the harp in London!

While London's famous Covent Garden oratories, under the direction of Sir Henry Bishop, featured twelve harpists headed by Dizi; Drury Lane, directed by Sir George Smart, included thirteen harpists, headed by the fabulous Bochsa. By 1823, Bochsa was professor of harp at the newly founded Royal Academy of Music in London. He was also secretary of the musical department, and a life governor of the Academy. In 1826, he was appointed conductor at the King's Theatre.

For the twenty years from 1817 to 1837, Bochsa delighted London with his annual concerts, and he was largely responsible for the great vogue of the harp. His "irregularities" however, caused him to be dismissed from the Royal Academy in 1827. Twelve years later he eloped with a charming young singer (wife of Sir Henry Bishop) and the couple toured Europe (with the exception of France), North and South America, and Australia, giving concerts for nearly twenty years. Bochsa died in Sydney, Australia, in 1856. Few of his all too numerous solo pieces for the harp are still played. However, Bochsa's Method for the harp, his Etudes, and his fame as an early virtuoso, will continue to command attention.

Elias Parish-Alvars was born in England, of Jewish ancestry, in 1808. He studied the harp with Bochsa, Labarre and Dizi. By 1825, he had received considerable recognition as a harpist of great talent. He toured the continent from 1831 to 1836, with great success; and traveled in the near East, from 1838 to 1841. In 1847, Parish-Alvars was appointed chamber harpist to the Austrian Emperor. The musician died only two years after this appointment.

Hector Berlioz, in his *Treatise on Modern Instrumentation and Orchestration*, designates Parish-Alvars as a harpist of extraordinary talents. Berlioz cites several examples of Parish-Alvars' clever use of the enharmonic possibilities of the harp, and also mentions the harpist's proposal of a triple action for the harp. This triple action would apply to only three pedals: the C, the F, and the G. A lower notch for these three pedals (below the sharp notch in the pedal box) and the tripling of the connecting mechanism in the neck, or harmonic-curve, would provide the harp with the three enharmonic tones that cannot be produced on the double action harp—C double sharp for D natural; F double sharp for G natural; and G double sharp for A natural. While this undoubtedly would further increase the compass of the harp, the subsequent mastery of a further pedal action might be too bewildering for general use.

ORCHESTRAL USE OF THE DOUBLE ACTION HARP—Parish-Alvars' suggested triple action for the harp was never realized in his lifetime—nor has it yet been attempted. However, the double action harp continued to be used as an orchestral instrument, and its importance increased during the latter half of the nineteenth century.

Liszt included the harp in nearly all of his orchestral works. Wagner made such demands upon the harp that as many as six harps were used in his Bayreuth Festival orchestra. Rossini and Verdi both included solos to be sung to the accompaniment of the harp alone, in their respective operas: "William Tell" and "Il Trovator"; as did Wagner in "Tannhäuser".

Of the later romanticists, Brahms used the harp only once —his "Requiem" requires two harps playing in unison. However, Richard Strauss, César Franck, Jan Sibelius, Gabriel Fauré and Camille Saint-Saëns, were among the composers who, by their inclusion of the harp in their compositions for orchestra, assured the instrument the permanent place it now occupies in the present-day symphony orchestra.

Tschaikowsky and Rimsky-Korsakov also used the harp to advantage in their orchestral works. While Debussy, foremost of the impressionists, found almost every phase of the harp admirably suited to his needs.

1

2

1. Erard harp in style of Louis XVI, late 19th century; made for the Emperor Franz Joseph of Austria. The instrument is a double action one, and has 47 strings; mechanism is gold plated.

2. Concert grand harp, made for Alberto Salvi, in 1914, by the Rudolph Wurlitzer Company. The exquisite column is over six feet in height, and is completely covered with gold leaf.

PLATE XV

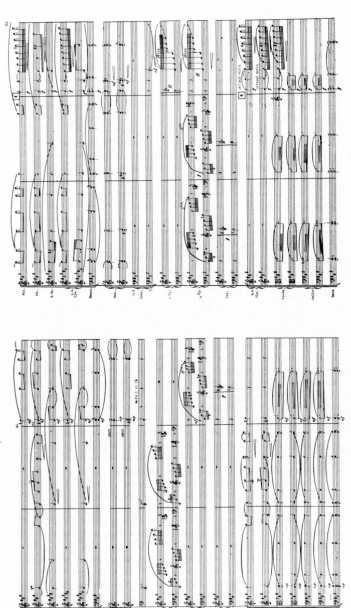

An example of modern orchestral writing for two harps—from score of "Sketches of the City," Op. 26, by Gardner Read. Pages 14 and 15. (Copyright 1938, Edwin A. Kalmus, Inc., N.Y.C.)

PLATE XVI

[54]

CHAPTER VI

Recorded Orchestral Works

THE FOLLOWING list is made up of recorded orchestral works by a variety of selected composers. The score of each of these compositions includes a part (or parts) for harp. It is hoped that by listening to some of these phonograph recordings the reader may obtain a better understanding of the orchestral use of the modern harp.

A miniature score, or the composer's score, will be found an invaluable aid for serious analytical listening. However, these compositions have been selected chiefly for the audibility of the harp part.

The record numbers listed are from current record catalogues. Many record libraries will include earlier recordings of these compositions. (Abbreviations: Columbia—C; Victor —V.)

Examples of orchestral use of the harp—listed alphabetically by specific effects. (For further information on special effects in harp music, see—Section II, Chapter VI):

ARPEGGIO—
    Liszt—"Les Preludes"
        London Symphony, Weingartner conducting—CM X198.
        Philadelphia Orchestra, Ormandy conducting—VM 453.
    Moussorgsky—"A Night on Bare Mountain"
        Philadelphia Orchestra, Stokowski conducting—V 17900.
    Wagner—"Isolde's Love-Death" from "Tristan and Isolde"
        Berlin Philharmonic, Furtwangler conducting—V 14935.

CADENZA—
    Rimsky-Korsakov—"Capriccio Espagnol"
        Boston "Pops" Orchestra, Fiedler conducting—V 11827/8.
        New York Philharmonic Symphony Orchestra, Barbirolli conducting—CM X185.

THE HARP

Thomas—Overture to "Mignon"
  N. B. C. Symphony Orchestra, Toscanini conducting—V
  11-8545.
Tschaikowsky—"Valse des Fleurs" from "Nutcracker Suite"
  Chicago Symphony Orchestra, Stock conducting—CM 395,
  (AM 395).
  Philharmonic Symphony Orchestra of New York, Rodzinski
  conducting—C 12385, Album CM 627.

CHORDS—

Franck—Second movement, third movement—"Symphony in D
  Minor"
    Minneapolis Symphony Orchestra, Mitropoulos conducting
    —VM 840.
    San Francisco Symphony Orchestra, Monteux conducting—
    CM X198.
Saint-Saëns—"Phaeton"
    Paris Conservatory Orchestra, Coppola conducting—V 11431.

CHORDS—ARPEGGIATED CHORDS—

Massenet—"Madrilene" from "Le Cid" Ballet Suite
    Boston "Pops" Orchestra, Fiedler conducting—V DM1058

GLISSANDO—

Debussy—"Prelude to the Afternoon of a Faun"
    London Symphony Orchestra, Beecham conducting—
    C 69600d.
    Philadelphia Orchestra, Stokowski conducting—V 17700.
Ravel—"Daphnis et Chloe" Suite No. II
    Boston Symphony Orchestra, Koussevitzky conducting—
    V 7143/4.
    Cleveland Symphony Orchestra, Rodzinski conducting—
    CM X230.
    Philadelphia Orchestra, Ormandy conducting—VM 667.
Respighi—"Fountains of Rome"
    New York Philharmonic Symphony Orchestra, Barbirollı
    conducting—VM 576.

HARMONICS—

Stravinsky—"Berceuse" from "Fire Bird" Suite
    N.B.C. Symphony Orchestra, Stokowski conducting—V
    DM993.
    New York Philharmonic Symphony Orchestra, Stokowski
    conducting—CM 653.

RECORDED ORCHESTRAL WORKS

TRILL—

Enesco—"Roumanian Rhapsody No. 1"
Chicago Symphony Orchestra, Stock conducting—C X-203.
Philadelphia Orchestra, Ormandy conducting—V 18201.

The harp as an accompaniment for solo instrument—

FLUTE AND HARP--

Bizet—"Menuetto" from "Arlesienne Suite No. II"
Boston "Pops" Orchestra, Fiedler conducting—VM 683.

VIOLA AND HARP—

Berlioz—"Harold in the Mountains"—first movement, "Harold in Italy"
Boston Symphony Orchestra, Koussevitzky conducting—V DM 989.

VIOLIN AND HARP—

Strauss—"Death and Transfiguration"
New York City Orchestra, Stokowski conducting—V DM1006.

Orchestral Use of Two Harps—

Berlioz—"A Ball"—second movement, "Symphonie Fantastique"
Cleveland Orchestra, Rodzinski conducting—CM 488.
San Francisco Symphony Orchestra, Monteux conducting—V DM 994.

Recorded Orchestral Works of Further Interest—

BACH-STOKOWSKI—"Sarabande" from 3rd English Suite for piano, freely transcribed by Stokowski
Philadelphia Orchestra, Stokowski conducting—V 16630 (Album DM 243).

BORODINE—"Deuxieme Symphonie"
Chicago Symphony Orchestra, Defauw conducting—V DM 1225.

CHABRIER—"Espana Rhapsodie"
Boston "Pops" Orchestra, Fiedler conducting—V 4375.
Detroit Symphony Orchestra, Gabrilowitsch conducting—V 1337.

DEBUSSY—"Iberia"
New York Philharmonic Symphony Orchestra, Barbirolli conducting—VM 460.
—"La Mer"

THE HARP

Boston Symphony Orchestra, Koussevitzky conducting—
VM 643.
Cleveland Orchestra, Rodzinski conducting—CM 531.
—"Nocturnes"
Philadelphia Orchestra, Stokowski conducting—VM 630.

IBERT—"Escales"—Port of Call
New York Philharmonic Symphony Orchestra, Rodzinski
conducting—CM X263.
San Francisco Symphony Orchestra, Monteux conducting—
V DM1178.

KALINNIKOW—"Premiere Symphony"
Indianapolis Symphony Orchestra, Sevitzky conducting—V
M/DM 827.

LIADOFF—"Enchanted Lake"
Boston Symphony Orchestra, Koussevitzky conducting—V
14078.

PROKOFIEFF—"Symphony No. 5"
Boston Symphony Orchestra, Koussevitzky conducting—VM
1095.
New York Philharmonic Symphony Orchestra, Rodzinski
conducting—CM 661.

RAVEL—"La Valse"
San Francisco Symphony Orchestra, Monteux conducting—
VM 820.

RESPIGHI—"Pines of Rome"
Paris Conservatory Orchestra, Coppola conducting—V
11917/8.
Philadelphia Orchestra, Ormandy conducting—CM 616.

RIMSKY-KORSAKOV—"Scheherazade" Symphonic Suite
Cleveland Orchestra, Rodzinski conducting—CM 398.
London Philharmonic Orchestra, Dorati conducting—VM
509.

SAINT-SAENS—"Danse Macabre"
Chicago Symphony Orchestra, Stock conducting—C 11251.
Philadelphia Orchestra, Stokowski conducting—V 14162.

SIBELIUS—"Symphony No. 1 in E Minor"
Minneapolis Symphony Orchestra, Ormandy conducting—
V 290.

RECORDED ORCHESTRAL WORKS

Philadelphia Orchestra, Ormandy conducting—V DM881.
Symphony Orchestra, Kajanus conducting—CM 151.
—"Valse Triste"
Chicago Symphony Orchestra, Stock conducting—V6579.
London Philharmonic Orchestra, Harty conducting—C 7322.
Philadelphia Orchestra, Stokowski conducting—V 14726.

SMETANA—"The Moldau"
Czech Philharmonic, Kubelik conducting—VM 523.
National Symphony, Kindler conducting—VM 921.

STRAUSS—"Don Juan"
London Philharmonic, Busch conducting—VM 351.
Pittsburgh Symphony Orchestra, Reiner conducting—CM X190.
—"Don Quixote"
New York Philharmonic Orchestra, Beecham conducting—VM 144.
Philadelphia Orchestra, Ormandy conducting—VM 720.

TSCHAIKOWSKY—"Aurora's Wedding" Ballet Suite
London Philharmonic, Kurtz conducting—V M326.
—"Romeo and Juliet" Overture
Boston Symphony Orchestra, Koussevitzky conducting—VM 347.
Cleveland Orchestra, Rodzinski conducting—CM 478.
—"Swan Lake" Ballet Suite
London Philharmonic Orchestra, Barbirolli conducting—V 11666/7.

Wagner—"Entrance of the Gods to Valhalla" from "Das Rheingold"
Bayreuth Festival Orchestra, Von Hosslin conducting—CM 338.
—"Magic Fire Music" from "Die Walkure"
Philadelphia Orchestra, Stokowski conducting—V 15800.
—"Die Meistersinger"
Saxon State Orchestra, Singers, Bohm conducting—V M537, AM537.
—"Tannhäuser"
Singers, Chorus and Bayreuth Festival Orchestra, Elmendorff conducting—CM 154.

CHAPTER VII

The "Chromatic" Harp

THE "DANCES—Sacred and Profane"[10] which Debussy composed for strings and harp, were originally written for the harp that was developed by Pleyel, Wolff & Company, in Paris. This harp is referred to as the "chromatic" harp. It was constructed on the principle of the piano, and was practically without mechanism.

In 1845, Henry Pape, a piano manufacturer, conceived the idea of constructing a harp that could provide the diatonic scale and the accidentals ("chromatics"), and yet be without pedals. His plans were not developed until M. Lyon, of Pleyel, Wolff & Company, became interested in the idea.

The "chromatic" harp as developed by this company, retained the general outline of the traditional harp, but employed *two* sets of strings, rather than one. The strings, running from the right side of the neck to the left side of the sounding-board, were white, and tuned in the diatonic scale of C major. The strings, running from the left side of the neck to the right side of the sounding-board, were black, and tuned to the accidentals. The two sets of strings crossed midway between the neck and the sounding-board. The provision of a string for each chromatic semi-tone, completely eliminated the necessity of foot pedals. The metal frame of the instrument obliged the strings to stay in tune almost as long as those of a piano.

Although much of the piano music that could not be played

---

[10] The "Dances" were first performed in Paris in 1904, by Mme. Wurmser-Delcourt. First American performances of the work were in 1916, with Carlos Salzedo as soloist; and in 1919 with Mme. Wurmser-Delcourt.

on the pedal harp, could be added to the repertoire of the "chromatic" harp, with the latter instrument it was necessary for the fingers to work on two different planes (rather than only one, as with the pedal harp, and the piano). Also, for obvious reasons, the tone of the Pleyel harp was found to be rather weak.

Three of these "chromatic" harps, from a group of two hundred and fifty manufactured in France, were brought to America by the celebrated harpist, Mme. Amelia Conti. The instruments, standing over six feet in height, were of maple wood, and were decorated with golden cupids and garlands. The number of strings was seventy-six, almost double the amount required by the average pedal harp.

An American-made "chromatic" harp is included in the Crosby Brown Collection of Musical Instruments. The harp, of maple wood, has *two* columns, each measuring five foot six inches in height, and the instrument is without pedals. There are 45 strings on the left side of the harp, tuned in "naturals". The strings of the right side number 33, and are tuned to the chromatic tones. These strings are arranged in groups of two and three, as are the black keys of the piano. This double-columned "chromatic" harp was built in the late 19th century by H. Greenway of Brooklyn, New York.

3

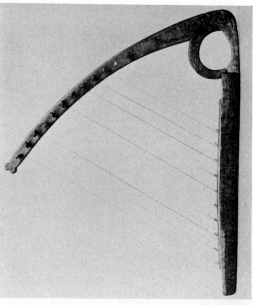

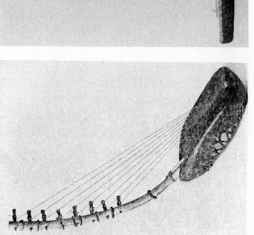

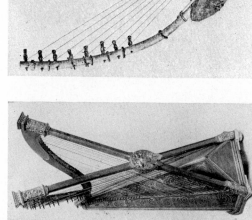

1. "Chromatic" or double harp, made by H. Greenway, Brooklyn, N. Y., late 19th century. Height of each pillar is 5 feet 6 inches.
Courtesy of the Metropolitan Museum of Art.

2. "Nanga" from Zanzibar. The primitive harp of the African natives.
Courtesy of the Metropolitan Museum of Art

3. Harp of the Ossetes (or Ossetines—an Indo-Germanic race dwelling in central Caucasus). The harp is 1 foot 10 inches in height; 2 feet in width. The 12 strings were of horse hair—each string consisting of 6 to 8 hairs. Note the absence of a fore-pillar, as with the early Eastern harps. This little harp was purchased for the Victoria and Albert Museum at the Paris Exhibition of 1867.
By Courtesy of the Victoria and Albert Museum.

[63]

PLATE XVII

Student harpists at the National Music Camp, Interlochen, Michigan, where every camper, who so desires, is given an opportunity to study the harp.

Courtesy of Dr. Joseph E. Maddy, president National Music Camp.

PLATE XVIII

CHAPTER VIII

The Pedal Harp In America

LYON & HEALY HARP—The Pleyel, Wolff & Co. harp was introduced in Europe eighty years after the Erard double action harp made its first appearance. It was also at this time that the first American-made harp was introduced to the old world. The European harps imported to America had included instruments by Erard, Erat, Dodd, Grosjean, Nadermann and Meyer. The first European harp probably reached the middle west sometime in the 1840's. As the population of the centrally located city of Chicago grew, the Lyon & Healy Music Company of that city became the largest importers of new and used European harps.

The increased demands for a harp that could better withstand the American climate, prompted Patrick J. Healy, founder of Lyon & Healy, and George B. Durkee, factory superintendent, to contemplate the possibilities of an American-made harp. Following two years of experimentation and investigation, and an initial cost of $10,000, the first Lyon & Healy harp was produced in 1889.

This new American harp included thirteen improvements—from more precise pedal action, to increased "hand room" in the upper octaves. The original harp first built by Lyon & Healy is still in use at Morgan Park high school in Chicago, Illinois.

PROMINENT NAMES IN THE HARP WORLD PRIOR TO 1900—A list of prominent names in the harp world at the time of the introduction of both the Lyon & Healy harp and the Pleyel, Wolff & Company instrument, would include the fol-

THE HARP

lowing artists: (listed alphabetically) Carl Alberstötter, Elvira
Atwood, Aptommas (who, it is said, played with the harp
resting on his left shoulder in the manner of the early Welsh
bards), Mme. Priscilla Aptommas, Melanie Bauer-Zeich, K.
Berg-Bachkarewa, A. Bertucat-Maretzek, Emma Weast Bichl,
A. Brietschuck-Marquardt, Inez Carusi, Esmeralde Cer-
vantes, John Cheshire, H. B. Fabiani, B. Fedorow, Jules
Franck, Alphonse Hasselmans, F. Lebano, Melba Messinger,
Maud Morgan, F. Moser, Otto Mosshammer, Clara Murray,
Heinrich Ohme, Franz Poenitz, Wilhelm Posse, Van Veachton
Rogers, Edmund Schuecker, Heinrich Schuecker, A. Serpkow,
Johannes Snoer, T. H. (Tommy) Wright, Margaretha Wun-
derle, and Anton Zamara.

WURLITZER HARP—In 1909, the Rudolph Wurlitzer Company began the manufacture of harps, in North Tonawanda,
New York. Among the new features of the Wurlitzer harp
was the use of maple ribs or braces (in the sounding-body)
rather than the non-vibrating metal ribs, previously employed.
An "anchor" (on the inside of the sounding-board) and
shoulder brace, were also developed to counteract the tremendous pull of nearly 2,000 pounds, to which the harp strings
subject the frame of the harp.

Outstanding features of the American-built harp were and
still are, the increased volume of the instrument, and the
greater durability of the harp, due to its more solid construction. The American-built harp of more recent times is also
notable for the veneered sounding-board, with the length-wise
use of the grain of the wood. In 1924, the American-built
harp (Wurlitzer) was endorsed by such musical greats as:
Rudolph Ganz, Walter Damrosch, Ossip Gabrilowitsch, Edwin Franko Goldman, Fritz Reiner, Henri Verbrugghen, and
Leopold Stokowski.

OUTSTANDING HARPISTS OF THE TWENTIES—The Wurlitzer
Harp catalogue of 1924, and the Lyon & Healy Harp catalogue of 1927, have provided the following list of names of

harpists appearing before the American public (in both solo and orchestral capacity) during this active period: (in alphabetical order)—Kajetan Attl, Winifred Bambrick, Lucille Johnson Bigelow, Winifred Carter, Theodore Cella, Zhay Clarke, Amelia Conti, Annie Louise David, Walter DeSota, Salvatore DeStefano, Vincent Fanelli, Harietta Gelfius, Margaret de Graff, Marcel Grandjany, Mary Butt Griffith, W. B. Griffith, Alfred Holy, Margaret Jiskra, Alfred Kastner, Lucile Lawrence, Dominic Mellillo, P. L. Montani, Marie Morgatt, Virginia Mulholland, Frank A. Nicoletta, Steffy Goldner Ormandy, Djina Ostrowska, Graziella Pampari, Carlo Pavese, A. F. Pinto, Joseph Pizzo, Giuseppi Quintile, Mildred Faulkner Rice, Virginia Rice, Gertrude Ina Robinson, Marie Roselli, M. A. Russo, Audrey Ryan, Alberto Salvi, Carlos Salzedo, Ada Sassoli, Philip Sevasta, Harriet Shaw, Carlos Sodero, Nell V. Steck, Clara Louise Thurston, Enrico Tramonti, Edward Vito, Joseph Vito, George W. Wheeler, Henry J. Williams, Bernard Zighera, and Nellie Zimmer.

Prominence came early to many of the aforementioned musicians, for a large number of them are still familiar names, as being among the outstanding artists of today's harp world.

CHAPTER IX

Future Opportunities

THE IMPROVEMENTS of the American-built harp have exerted their influence on both the fields of composition and of performance. The composers of the 20th century have been able to write for the harp as a bona fide member of the orchestra, and not as a thin-voiced prima donna.

On the concert stage the harp has not enjoyed the prevalence of the piano, the violin or the voice, because the number of concert harpists is so very small, in comparison to the tremendous number of concert pianists, violinists and singers, both in Europe and America. However, the 20th century *has* provided a field for the harp virtuoso. In seven consecutive concert seasons, Alberto Salvi, the Italian-born virtuoso, played more than 1,000 concerts in tours extending across the continent from Canada and the United States, to Cuba and Porto Rico. Three hundred of these concerts were presented without the assistance of other artists.

The influx of French, Italian, English and German musicians to this country, during the latter part of the nineteenth century and the early part of the present century, provided America with an outstanding group of competent and highly trained European orchestral and concert harpists. These musicians have been of prime importance in the molding of the American-born harpists of the later generations.

Prior to World War I, and in the years between World wars I and II, many young American-born harpists received at least a part of their musical education in Europe. Thus, in two ways, many of the best features of the European schools of harp playing are now available to the present generation of American harp students in their *own* country.

AMERICAN SCHOOLS—An outstanding example of the success of harp instruction in America is offered by the graduates of the Curtis Institute of Music in Philadelphia, Pennsylvania. The Curtis harp department was founded in 1924 by Carlos Salzedo. By 1937, six of the Curtis harp graduates to achieve prominence in the musical world were: Florence Wightman, as first harpist Metropolitan Opera Association; Casper Reardon, as first harpist Cincinnati Symphony; Edna Phillips,[11] as first harpist Philadelphia Orchestra; Marjorie Tyre, as alternating first harpist Philadelphia Orchestra; Marjorie Call, as first harpist Indianapolis Symphony Orchestra; and Alice Chalifoux, as first harpist of the Cleveland Orchestra.

Since 1938, Marcel Grandjany, first head of the harp department of France's well-known Fontainebleau School of Music for American Students (established 1921), has been the head of the harp department of New York City's Juilliard School of Music.

An increasingly large number of American colleges, universities, and music conservatories (as well as a number of high schools throughout the country), offer harp instruction or courses in the study of the harp. While space does not permit a complete listing of these schools, the following are included as among those providing the foremost instruction to harp students in America: (listed alphabetically)

AMERICAN CONSERVATORY OF MUSIC
   Chicago, Illinois
     Harp department—Margaret Sweeney.
ARTHUR JORDAN CONSERVATORY OF MUSIC
   (Affiliated with Butler University)
   1204 North Delaware Street, Indianapolis, Indiana

---

11 With Grace Weymer and Eleanor Shaffner, compiler of a four year harp course for high school music credit.

FUTURE OPPORTUNITIES

Harp department—Mary Spalding, harpist, Indianapolis Symphony Orchestra.

CARNEGIE INSTITUTE OF TECHNOLOGY
College of Fine Arts—Music Department
Schenley Park, Pittsburgh, Pennsylvania
   Harp department—Edward Druzinsky, harpist, Pittsburgh Symphony Orchestra.

CHICAGO MUSICAL COLLEGE
Chicago, Illinois
Harp department—Marie Ludwig.

CINCINNATI CONSERVATORY OF MUSIC
(Affiliated with University of Cincinnati)
Highland and Oak Street, Cincinnati, Ohio
   Harp department—Anna Bukay, harpist, Cincinnati Symphony Orchestra.

CLEVELAND INSTITUTE OF MUSIC
2605 Euclid Avenue, Cleveland, Ohio
   Harp department—Alice Chalifoux, harpist, Cleveland Symphony Orchestra.

COLUMBIA UNIVERSITY, MUSIC DEPARTMENT
New York, New York
Harp department—Carlos Salzedo.

CURTIS INSTITUTE OF MUSIC
Rittenhouse Square, Philadelphia, Pennsylvania
Harp department—Carlos Salzedo.

DETROIT INSTITUTE OF MUSICAL ART
(Affiliated with University of Detroit)
52 Putnam Avenue, Detroit, Michigan
Harp department—Ann Sacchi.

JUILLIARD SCHOOL OF MUSIC
120 Claremont Avenue, New York, New York.
Harp department—Marcel Grandjany.

MILLS COLLEGE, SCHOOL OF FINE ARTS—MUSIC DEPARTMENT
Oakland, California
   Harp department—Virginia Morgan Robinson, harpist, San Francisco Symphony Orchestra.

NEW ENGLAND CONSERVATORY OF MUSIC
Huntington Avenue, Boston, Massachusetts
   Harp department—Bernard Zighera, harpist, Boston Symphony Orchestra.

THE HARP

NORTHWESTERN UNIVERSITY, SCHOOL OF MUSIC
Evanston, Illinois
Harp department—Alberto Salvi.

OBERLIN COLLEGE, CONSERVATORY OF MUSIC
Oberlin, Ohio
Harp department—Lucy Lewis.

PEABODY CONSERVATORY OF MUSIC
Mt. Vernon Place and Charles Street, Baltimore, Maryland
Harp department—Giuseppe Pizzo, harpist, Baltimore Symphony Orchestra.

PHILADELPHIA CONSERVATORY OF MUSIC
216 South 20th Street, Philadelphia, Pennsylvania
Harp department—Edna Phillips.

PHILADELPHIA MUSICAL ACADEMY
1617 Spruce Street, Philadelphia, Pennsylvania
Harp department—Stephanie Ormandy.

ROCHESTER UNIVERSITY, EASTMAN SCHOOL OF MUSIC
Rochester, New York
Harp department—Eileen Malone, harpist, Rochester Civic
Orchestra and Rochester Philharmonic Orchestra.

ROOSEVELT COLLEGE
Chicago, Illinois
Harp department—Grace Weymer Follet.

ST. LOUIS INSTITUTE OF MUSIC
St. Louis, Missouri
Harp department—Graziella Pampari, harpist, St. Louis
Symphony Orchestra.

STEPHENS COLLEGE (Junior College for Women)
Conservatory of Music
Columbia, Missouri
Harp department—Muretta Meyer Henderson

UNIVERSITY OF MICHIGAN, SCHOOL OF MUSIC
Ann Arbor, Michigan
Harp department—Priscilla Jean Eitel.

UNIVERSITY OF SOUTHERN CALIFORNIA, INSTITUTE OF THE ARTS
3551 University Avenue, Los Angeles, California
Lecturer in Harp—Catherine Jackson.

UNIVERSITY OF TEXAS, COLLEGE OF FINE ARTS—MUSIC DEPT.
Austin, Texas
Harp department—Mary Masters Mylecraine.

[72]

FUTURE OPPORTUNITIES

WARD BELMONT SCHOOL (Junior College, Preparatory School
and Conservatory of Music for Young Women)
Belmont Heights, Nashville, Tennessee
Harp department—Frances Jackson Parker.

THE CIVIC ORCHESTRA OF CHICAGO—Unique opportunity for
the study of the harp is offered by the Civic orchestra of
Chicago, training school for young musicians, conducted by
the Chicago symphony orchestra. This outstanding organization
not only offers the opportunity for actual playing experience
with an orchestra, but also includes harp sectional rehearsals
under the guidance of Joseph Vito, solo harpist of the Chicago
symphony orchestra.

SUMMER HARP STUDY—The opportunity for summer study of
the harp is available at many of the aforementioned schools.
There are also a number of outstanding music camps which
offer harp instruction. Probably the best known of these camps
is the *National Music Camp,* Interlochen, Michigan (affiliated
with the University of Michigan). The National Music Camp's
extensive summer program includes both private and class
instruction for all campers who wish to study the harp.

The Berkshire Music Center (founded in 1940 by Dr.
Koussevitzky and the Boston symphony orchestra) at Tangle-
wood, Lenox, Massachusetts, offers the opportunity for music
study in connection with the Berkshire Festival Concerts.
Applicants are selected by audition, and the enrollment of
harpists is limited to a few advanced students, already equipped for orchestral and ensemble work.

The Summer Harp Colony of America was established at
Camden, Maine in 1931 by Carlos Salzedo. The colony offers
harp instruction by Salzedo, combined with the interesting
features of a summer in Maine, as well as the opportunity to
meet leading harpists who are exponents of the Salzedo
method.

THE HARP IN SCHOOL MUSIC—The question of who should
play the harp frequently arises in connection with the school

owned instruments. The answer is—anyone with a love of the instrument and a genuine desire to learn. The initial expense of the instrument, and the upkeep (chiefly the purchase of harp strings), has placed the harp in a prohibitive class for many people. This is all the more reason why the school-owned instrument should be made available to several students each year. The school music director who becomes discouraged by the "turn-over" of harp students, needs only to consider the number of high school orchestra concert-masters that will be developed from a grade school violin class.

It must be realized that several years study of the harp does not insure a permanent career with the instrument, but much pleasure can be derived. Those students who wish to become professional harpists must practice the harp quite as diligently as they would practice any other musical instrument. A background of some previous music—especially the study of the piano—will be found most helpful. The technique of the fingers, and efficient use and understanding of the pedals must be developed. An accurate sense of pitch is also of utmost importance. The student must always bear in mind that the present day professional harpist must be a musician of the first rank.

Opportunities for the harp are limitless in the ever-widening scope of the musical world. The symphony, opera, theatre and ballet orchestras; motion pictures; radio, and television; and the field of teaching; all are open to the competent musician.

CHAPTER X

Selected Bibliography

THE FOLLOWING BIBLIOGRAPHY is presented to acquaint the reader with the interesting and picturesque material that is available concerning the harp. The Bibliography has been divided into four general divisions:

I—General Information
II—Ancient Harp
III—Old English, Irish, Welsh and Highland Harps
IV—Foreign Language Works

The books and articles listed in the first division include: histories of all the harp forms; repertoire; biographies of harpists; harp collections; and fundamental information. The second and third divisions contain books of a more specialized nature.

Most school and public libraries own several of the books which are included in the General Information division. It is hoped that even the smallest of these libraries will also include at least one of the books or articles mentioned in the other divisions.

The musical encyclopedias, and reference books, common to every library will naturally offer a source of general information on the harp. Further material can also be found in books on orchestration, books or brochures about specific symphony orchestras, and symphony orchestra programs. The latter, bound in yearly volumes, offer an excellent criteria of the concert repertoire for the harp.

THE HARP

I—General Information

COBBET'S CYCLOPEDIC SURVEY OF CHAMBER MUSIC—Milford. London. Oxford University Press. 1929. Vol. I. Pages 509-511. The Harp. Article by Maud C. Korchinka and C. Kony.
Pages 404-405. Flute and Harp. Article by L. Fleury.

A FAMOUS COLLECTION—Article on the Crosby Brown Musical Instrument Collection, Metropolitan Museum, New York City.
"Hobbies" magazine. July 1943.
Pages 10-11. Chicago. Lightner Press.

FAMOUS HARPIST COLLECTS HARPS—Article on the harp collection of Mildred Dilling.
"Hobbies" magazine. May 1938.
Page 28. Chicago. Lightner Press.

THE HARP AS A CAREER—Conference with Elaine Vito, by Myles Fellows.
"Etude" magazine. November 1947.
Page 609, 660. Philadelphia. Presser.

THE HARP AS A SOLO INSTRUMENT AND IN THE ORCHESTRA—By Alfred Kastner. Proceedings of the Musical Association, (1908-1909).
Pages 1-14. London. Novello & Co., Ltd. 1909.

THE HARP IN COLLEGE AND UNIVERSITY TRAINING—Conference with Lucy Lewis and Carlos Salzedo, by Gunnar Asklund.
"Etude" magazine. February 1946.
Pages 67, 68. Philadelphia. Presser.

HARPS—Article on the collection of harps and harp objects of Virginia Morgan.
"Hobbies" magazine. September 1945.
Page 9. Chicago. Lightner Press.

HISTORY OF MUSICAL INSTRUMENTS—Curt Sachs.
New York. W. W. Norton. 1940.
See Index for numerous references to the harp.

HISTORY OF THE HARP—John Thomas.
London. Hutchings & Romer. 19 Pages.

SELECTED BIBLIOGRAPHY

INSTRUMENTS OF THE MODERN ORCHESTRA—Kathleen Schlesinger.
London.   W. Reeves.   1910.   Volume I.
Pages 138-147.   The Harp.
Pages 148-149.   Two New Harps.
Pages 150-153.   Chromatic Harp.

LESLIE LINDSEY MASON COLLECTION OF MUSICAL INSTRUMENTS —Article on collection housed at Boston Museum of Fine Arts.
"Hobbies" magazine.   June 1943.
Page 16.   Chicago.   Lightner Press.

LYON & HEALY HARP CATALOGUE (1900 edition)—Printed by Donnelley & Sons for Lyon & Healy Inc.

MODERN ORCHESTRATION AND INSTRUMENTS—Henri Kling, translated by Gustav Saenger.
New York.   Carl Fischer.   1902.
Pages 50-60.   The Harp.

MUSICAL INSTRUMENTS—Karl Geiringer, translated by Bernard Miall.
New York.   Oxford University Press.   1945.
See Index for numerous references to the harp.

MUSICAL MYTHS AND FACTS—Carl Engel.
London.   Novello, Ewer & Company.   1876.
Pages 32-73.   Collection of Musical Instruments (in Europe).

THE ORCHESTRA AND ITS INSTRUMENTS—Esther Singleton.
New York.   The Symphony Society of New York.   1917.
Pages 279-289.   The Harp.

ORCHESTRATION—Cecil Forsyth.
London.   Macmillan & Co., Stainer & Bell.   1929 (1914).
Pages 461-475.   The Harp.
Pages 476-477.   Chromatic Harp.

ORCHESTRAL INSTRUMENTS AND THEIR USE—Arthur Elson.
Boston.   L. C. Page & Company.   1903.
Pages 106-126.   The Harp.

OXFORD COMPANION TO MUSIC—Edited by Percy Scholes.
2nd American Edition.   1943.   Oxford University Press.
Pages 410-413.   The Harp.

ROMANCE OF THE HARP—Article by Annie W. Patterson.
"Etude" magazine.   October 1929.
Pages 731-732.   Philadelphia.   Presser.

THE STORY OF THE HARP—W. H. G. Flood.
London.   Walter Scott, New York.   Scribner's.   1905.
199 Pages.

TINY HARPS—Article on the collection of miniature harps made
by Mrs. C. H. Rensch.
"Hobbies" magazine.   July 1942.
Page 112.   Chicago.   Lightner Press.

TREATISE ON MODERN INSTRUMENTATION AND ORCHESTRA-
TION—Hector Berlioz, translated by Mary Cowden Clarke.
London.   Novello & Company.
Pages 61-66.   The Harp.

WHO IS WHO IN MUSIC—1941 Edition.
Chicago.   Lee Stern Press.
Pages 482-483.   The Harp.   Article by Carlos Salzedo.
Pages 31-247.   Biographical section includes current harp-
ists.

WURLITZER HARP CATALOGUE—(1924 Edition).
Printed for the Wurlitzer Company.

II—Ancient Harp

MUSICAL INSTRUMENTS—Carl Engel.
Published for the Committee of Council on Education by
Chapman & Hall, 193 Piccadilly, 1875, London. Reprints
of material appearing in the Museum of South Kensington
Catalogues.
See Index for the numerous references to the early harp
forms, throughout the book.

MUSIC OF ANTIQUITY—Article by Charles N. Lanphere.
"Hobbies" magazine.   September 1938.
Pages 15-17.   Chicago.   Lightner Press.

POPULAR HISTORY OF MUSIC—W. S. B. Mathews.
Chicago.   "Music" Magazine Publishing Co.   1891.
Revised 1906.
Pages 27-39.   Music among the ancient Egyptians.
Pages 40-47.   Music among the ancient Hebrews and
Assyrians.
Pages 48-69.   Music among the ancient Greeks.

SELECTED BIBLIOGRAPHY

RISE OF MUSIC IN THE ANCIENT WORLD—Curt Sachs.
New York.   W. W. Norton.   1943.
See Index for the numerous references to the ancient harp
forms, throughout the book.

III—Old English, Irish, Welsh and Highland Harps

AN HISTORICAL ENQUIRY—Respecting the Performance on the
Harp in the Highlands of Scotland; From Earliest Times
Until it was Discontinued—1734—By John Gunn (1765-
1825).
Edinburgh.   A. Constable.   1807.   112 Pages.

ANNALS OF THE IRISH HARPERS—Charlotte M. Fox.
New York.   E. P. Dutton.   1912.   320 Pages.

DICTIONARY OF OLD ENGLISH MUSIC AND MUSICAL INSTRU-
MENTS—Edited by Jeffery Pulver.
New York.   Dutton.   1923.
Pages 99-102.   The Harp.

ENGLISH AND IRISH INSTRUMENTS—Robert Bruce Armstrong.
Edinburgh.   Constable & Co.   1908.
Pages 145-148.   Egan's Portable Harp.

502 OLD WELSH AIRS—Collected by N. Bennett, with twelve
portraits of old Welsh harpers and short accounts of their
lives.
London.   W. Reeves.   198 Pages.

HISTORICAL MEMORIES OF IRISH BARDS—Joseph Cooper Walker.
Dublin.   White.   1789.

HISTORY OF IRISH MUSIC—W. H. G. Flood.
Dublin.   Browne & Nolan Ltd.   1902.   357 Pages.
2nd Edition—Information throughout concerning the harp.

IRISH AND HIGHLAND HARPS—Robert Bruce Armstrong.
Edinburgh.   D. Douglas.   1904.   192 Pages.
Pages 1-54.   Irish Harps.
Pages 139-158.   Highland Harps.

MUSICAL AND POETICAL RELIKS OF THE WELSH BARDS—
Edward Jones.
London.   Printed by the author, 1794.   183 Pages.

[79]

THE HARP

MUSICAL INSTRUMENTS—Historical and Rare—A. J. Hipkins.
London.   A. & C. Black Ltd.   1921.
First published in 1888.
Plate II—Queen Mary's Harp.
Plate III—The Lamont Harp.
Plate XXXIV—Pedal Harp.

OLD ENGLISH INSTRUMENTS OF MUSIC—Francis W. Galpin.
Chicago.   McClurg.
London.   Mathews.   1911.
Pages 1-19.   Harp and Rote.

STORY OF BRITISH MUSIC—Frederick J. Crowest.
New York.   Scribner's Sons.   1896.   396 Pages.
See Index for the numerous references to the harp, through-
out the book.

IV—Foreign Language Works

L'ARPA—Riccardo Ruta.
Napolia, stabilimento tip. librari A. E. S. Festo 1901.

ENCYCLOPEDIE DE LA MUSIQUE ET DICTIONNAIRE DU CON-
SERVATOIRE.
Paris.   Librairie Delagrave.   1927.   Deuxieme Partie.
Technique de la Musique—Instruments à vent à cordes,
etc.
LA HARPE—*Pages* 1892-1971.
Des Origines au commencement du dix septième siècle—
par Marc Pincherle (p. 1892-1927).
La Harpe et sa Facture—par M. A. Blondel, Director de
la Maison Erard (p. 1928-1934).
La Harpe et sa Technique—par Alphonse Hasselmans-
Tournier (p. 1935-1941).
La Harpe Chromatique et sa Facture—par Gustave Lyon,
Director de la Maison Pleyel (p. 1942-1967).
La Harpe Chromatique et sa Technique—par Mme. Renée
Lenars, Professeur au conservatoire (p. 1968-1971).

HARFE UND HARFENSPIEL—Hans Joachim Zingel (1904).
Halle.   M. Niemeyer.

HARFE UND LYRE IN ALTEN NORDEUROPA—Hortense Panum.
Magazine of "International Musical Society" Leipzig, 1904.

SECTION II

FUNDAMENTALS

"The harp is an instrumente of swete meloyde,
Rude intelligens of the sounde conceyvethe no armonye,

But who so in that instrumente hathe no speculation,
What restithe withyn the sounde borde hathe but smale
probacion."

LEKINGFELDE PROVERB
(temp. Henry VII)

SECTION II

Fundamentals

THE FOLLOWING CHAPTER on Fundamentals was originally prepared as a "guide book" for the music education student— to provide the future band, orchestra, and choral conductors of the public school system with a basic knowledge of the harp. This knowledge should provide a three-fold benefit:

(1) The modern harp may be more intelligently and extensively employed in the school music system.

(2) The energies of the school harp students and would-be students can be directed along the most productive channels.

(3) With the proper care, the instrument purchased or rented for the school music department, will remain in playing condition for a greater length of time.

Harp in the public high school—The Symphony Orchestra of the J. Sterling Morton High School, Cicero, Illinois, Mr. Louis M. Blaha, conductor.

Courtesy of the J. Sterling Morton High School.

[85]

PLATE XIX

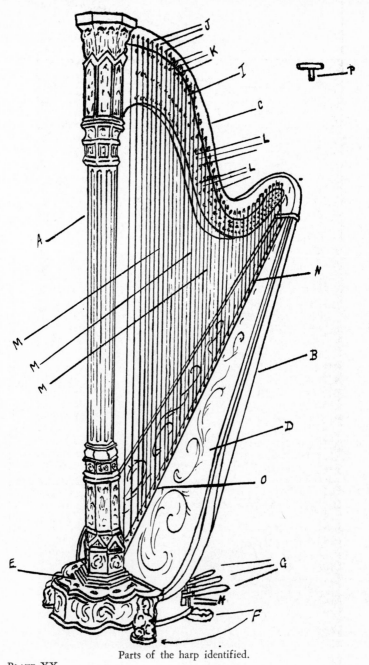

Parts of the harp identified.

PLATE XX

[86]

Parts of the Harp

A. Column, or fore-pillar, containing the seven pedal rods

B. Body of the harp

C. Curving neck, or harmonic curve

D. Sounding-board (large concert size)

E. Base of the harp

F. Feet

G. Pedals

H. Pedal notches

I. Metal plate concealing the mechanism

J. Tuning-pins

K. Rest-pins or bridge-pins

L. Rotating discs

M. Harp strings (gut and wire)

N. Ivory pegs

O. Eyelets (in sounding-board)

P. Tuning key

CHAPTER II

The Tonal Range and the Tuning of the Harp

THE TONAL RANGE of the modern harp (large concert size) encompasses six and one-half octaves—from contra-octave C (♭) to four-lined octave G (♯). The range of the smaller harps (46 strings; 41 strings) is generally from contra-octave D (♭) to four-lined G (♯); or from contra-octave G (♭) to four-lined E (♯).

CLEFS—Both the treble clef (𝄞) and the bass clef (𝄢) are used; as with piano music, the notation for the right hand is generally in the treble clef, and that for the left hand is generally in the bass clef.

TUNING—The harp strings are pitched diatonically. The harp is tuned in perfect octaves and almost perfect fifths; in the key of C flat, or the key of C natural (all the pedals depressed to the intermediate position). The strings are plucked firmly with the fingers of the left hand, while the key (or tuner) is manipulated by the right hand.

The tuning-pins should be turned slowly and pushed in tight (never *hammered* in), to prevent the pins from slipping back. The beginner may tune every string to the corresponding note on the piano, or pitch-pipe. Students must be encouraged to tune the harp frequently and accurately.

CHAPTER III

Harp Strings

THE STRINGS of the upper and middle octaves are made from the intestines of sheep,[12] but are commonly referred to as "cat-gut" strings. The strings currently come in three color-combinations:

C—green; F—purple; D, E, G, A and B—red

    or

C—red; F—purple; D, E, G, A and B—white

    or

C—red; F—purple; D, E, G, A and B—green.

The bass strings, from small-octave G or F, are of wound wire; the C and F strings are wound in copper, for better visibility.

HOW TO PURCHASE—Harp strings may be purchased by octave, name and number. The strings are numbered—commencing with four-lined E as number one. The octaves are counted from the highest strings—four-lined E commencing the first octave. Thus, the one-lined A string (440 A) would be identified as: third octave A string, number nineteen. Harp strings are sold individually, or in sets (gut or nylon set; wire set).

HOW TO PUT ON—To put on a gut string: thread the string through its eyelet in the sounding-board (having first removed

---

12 Nylon is the newest material for harp strings.

the ivory peg, if there was one) ; tie the end of the string in a double-loop knot:

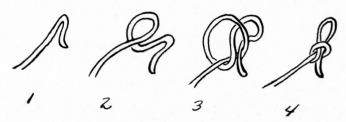

1   *2*   *3*   *4*

inserting a fifth octave string end for added support; knot the string once or even twice more, and carefully pull the string up, until the knot prevents further pull. (The string may be slackened to permit the return of the ivory peg—being careful to fit the grooved side of the peg to the string). The other end of the string is threaded through the hole in the tuning-pin; the tuning-pin is then turned by the harp tuning-key, ("key"; "tuner") until the string reaches the desired pitch. Most beginner's Method books have instructions for this; each harp instructor usually has an individual preference for the manner of bringing the string up to pitch. (In stringing the harp, care must be taken to keep each string in the ridge provided in the bridge-pin.)

The wire string comes with a ready-made "knot". Because the wire string is so much less pliable than the gut string, it is more difficult to put on without breaking. After being threaded through the sounding-board eyelet, and the tuning-pin, the wire string must be held quite loose, before the tuning process is started.

EFFECT OF TEMPERATURE ON STRINGS—The harp strings are affected by changes in temperature, just as the strings of other musical instruments. Rainy weather, drafts, etc. have an adverse effect on the strings. When the school harp is not in use it should be left covered with the harp cover. When the harp has been out of use for a long period of time the strings should be brought up to pitch *very* slowly.

CARE OF THE STRINGS—If the harp is to be stored in its trunk during the summer vacation, it is advisable to lower all the strings. At all times the surplus string-ends should be cut short and not left "waving" along the neck of the harp.

Any fuzzing on the strings may be clipped off with a manicure scissors.

It is possible to patch broken gut strings of the middle octaves. This can be done by over-lapping the original string and the patch string, and double-knotting them.

Chapter IV

Position

WHILE THE EXACT POSITION of the player at the harp must be established by the individual harp instructor, a few general remarks may aid the school music teacher in the guidance of the harp student's work in school music. (The orchestra or band director frequently sees the student "in action" more often during the week than does the harp instructor.) The beginner and student should be encouraged to maintain a correct position at the harp at all times.

OF THE INSTRUMENT—When in use, the harp rests on the right shoulder, and the inner sides of the knees, of the player. The instrument is inclined towards the player to such an extent that only its two rear feet remain on the ground.

OF THE CHAIR, OR BENCH, AND MUSIC STAND—The height of the chair, or bench, used should correspond to the proportions of the player and the size of the instrument. Beginners should be cautioned against sitting either too close or too far from the harp. The music stand, adjusted to its proper height, is placed to the left of the harp, within easy reach of the player's left hand.

OF THE PLAYER—The player should sit in an erect position, on a firm chair (a chair *without* arms) or bench. The body must be neither too tense nor too relaxed:

> *Feet*—When not in use, the feet should remain flat on the floor.

> *Hands*—It is generally agreed that the hands should be held in a curved position, with the knuckles curving out.

POSITION

The left hand plays slightly lower on the strings than the right hand.

Fingers—The finger-nails should be kept short. (At all times!) Only thumb, index, third and fourth fingers are used in harp playing, the fifth finger being too short for practical use.

It is of prime importance that the thumbs are placed in an upright position, and that careful attention is paid to the placing of all the fingers at all times. Beginners, if not carefully instructed, frequently underestimate the importance of the hand position and finger placement. This negligence may result in a poor hand position which hampers the tone production, and which must be *unlearned* rather than corrected.

The beginner (especially older beginners with technical facility on other musical instruments) must not be allowed to *snatch* at the harp strings, or to grasp the strings haphazardly, letting the fingers strike anywhere just to produce a sound. The technique of the harp is a specific one, and it is only through careful and diligent practice, with a trained instructor, that this technique can be adequately comprehended and developed.

Arms—The position of the arms varies from an absolutely horizontal one, to one of moderately raised elbows, again according to the instructor's preferred method. The right arm is generally permitted to touch the right side of the sounding-board; while the left arm should not come in contact with the sounding-board, except of necessity in the highest octaves (or for special effects). At no time should the student be permitted to *lean* on the sounding-board while playing.

CHAPTER V

Pedals

AS HAS BEEN STATED, the harp strings are tuned in the diatonic scale. The harp therefore has seven pedals corresponding to the seven different tones of the diatonic scale—C, D, E, F, G, A and B. The pedals are arranged at the base of the harp in the following order:

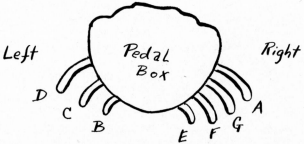

SINGLE ACTION—When the pedals were first added to the harp, the connecting mechanism (see Section I, Chapters III and IV) enabled each pedal, when depressed, to raise the string with which it was connected, by one semi-tone, through all the different octaves. (That is: C pedal connected to all C strings; D pedal, to all D strings; etc.)

While the addition of pedals to the harp greatly advanced the musical possibilities of the instrument, it was not yet possible to play in all the desired keys. If the harp was tuned in the key of C♭, the pedals could provide only the necessary chromatic changes through to the key of C♮. (If tuned in C♮ then only through to the key of C♯). Therefore, the single action harp was usually tuned in the key of E♭ major, making the keys of C, D, G, A, F, B♭ and E♭ possible. Many of the older European harps now in this country, and harps first made here at the turn of the century, are limited single-action instruments.

DOUBLE ACTION—Patented by Sebastian Erard in 1809, the "double action" added another set of notches to the pedal box. When the pedals were depressed to the intermediate position, the harp strings were raised (through all the octaves) by a semi-tone. A full depression of the pedals raised the strings yet another semi-tone; thus making the complete distance from the first notch to the third, that of a whole-tone.

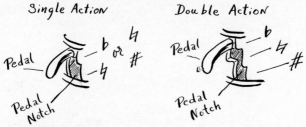

Because of this improvement, it is now possible to play in all major and minor keys.

The beginner and student must learn to move the pedals of the harp *silently*. Buzzing can be avoided with reasonable care.

EIGHTH PEDAL—This pedal may still be found on some old instruments. The function of the eighth pedal was to be similar to that of the damper pedal of the piano. Placed at the base of the harp, just to the right of the B pedal, the damper pedal controlled shutters fitted in the sound holes. (The sound holes run along the back of the body of the harp.) When it was found that the opening and closing of these shutters did not produce the desired effect, they were abandoned; many shutters already installed were removed and the eighth pedal notches plugged.

CHAPTER VI

Harp *Music and Special Effects*

Harp music may consist of:

SCALES—

Example from "Concerto in B*b*" by Handel-Grandjany, page 11.

(*Durand & Cie*)

ARPEGGIOS—

Example from "Legende" by Renie, page 17.

(*L. Rouhier*)

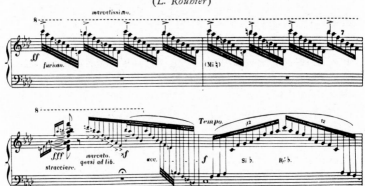

CHORDS—

Example from "Danse Sacrée" by Debussy, page 1.

(*Durand & Cie*)

ARPEGGIATED CHORDS (*indicated by a wavy line preceding the chord*)—

Example from "Fantasia Drammatica" by Sodero, page 3.

(*International Music Pub. Co.*)

OCTAVES—

Example from "On stilts" from *Short Stories in Music*
(second series), by Salzedo, page 3.

(Elkan-Vogel)

The *Tremolo* (for one or two hands); and such embellish-
ments as: the *Mordent,* the *Turn,* and the *Appoggiatura,*
are also possible on the harp.

BISBIGLIANDO—*Murmuring effect*
Example from "Will-o'-the-wisp", Hasselmans, page 1.
(*Schirmer*)

THE TRILL—*One hand*

Written thus:

Played thus:

or also:

THE HARP
—*Two hands*

Played thus:

Analogous to the execution of the shake, such passages must be mentioned here, in which two neigh-boring strings are produced unisono, with the aid of a pedal, for instance:—

here all A flats marked thus – are played by G sharp, and the E flats by D sharp.

Examples from *Universal Method,* Bochsa-Oberthur, pages 72 and 73.
(*Carl Fischer*)

DYNAMIC EFFECTS—*crescendo, diminuendo, etc.*—are achieved by pressure of the fingers, when playing (plucking) the strings.

The harp strings must be muffled when their vibration interferes with the following harmonies. This is done with the hands. Muffling of a specific string or strings—etouffé —is done by the hands or fingers, and is usually clearly indicated in the more recently published music for the harp.

ETOUFFÉ—

     —to muffle string vibration.

     —to muffle wire string vibration.

◇—to muffle a specific string.

PRÈS DE LA TABLE—

The effect obtained by playing close to the sounding-board of the harp—près de la table—is frequently called for in the classical transcriptions for harp. It is indicated by word, and (or) ﹈〜〜〜 . (Appearing above staff for r. h.; below staff for l. h.; between, for both hands.)

ETOUFFÉ and PRÈS DE LA TABLE—

Example from "La Commère" by Couperin, from *Transcrip-*
tions Classiques, by Grandjany, page 12.

(*Marks*)

The Bochsa-Oberthur *Universal Method*, also lists as effects:
guitar sounds; cithern sounds; and the sounds produced by
pressure of the pedals. The *Method for the harp*, Lawrence-
Salzedo, lists: vibrant sounds; anvil effects; and rolling
surf effects. Still other effects, discovered by Salzedo, are
to be found in his *Modern study of the harp*.

THE HARMONIC is one of the most attractive of the effects produced on the harp. It is usually indicated in the musical
score by a circle (o) placed directly above the desired
note or chord. The first harmonic (that of the octave) is
the one most generally used. The second harmonic (the
12th) is also possible on the harp. A single harmonic note
can be produced by either the right hand or the left hand.
Double and triple harmonics (chords) are most feasible
for the left hand. Unless otherwise indicated in the music,
the harmonic is written an octave lower than it is to sound.

THE HARP

Example from "Féerie" by Tournier, page 1.

(*L. Roubier*)

THE GLISSANDO is a characteristic effect of the modern pedal harp. It is achieved by a finger slide (either one, two, or three fingers are possible, with either hand) either up or down the strings. All the notes of the glissando may be printed in the music, or the glissando may be designated by a straight line connecting the highest and the lowest notes. Various combinations of the pedals will provide a glissando of: the dominant seventh chord; augmented, or diminished seventh chord; whole tone scale; etc. (For best results in writing glissandos for the harp the composer or arranger is advised to include pedal combination, or diagram, with each new glissando.)

Example from "Impromptu" by Fauré, page 5.

(*Durand & Cie*)

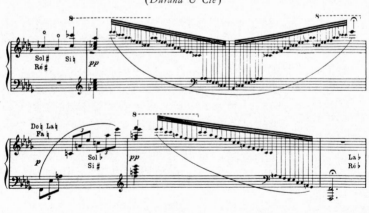

CHAPTER VII

Care of the Harp

IF THE HARP is to be moved any distance (out of the school building, etc.) it should be covered with the harp cover and placed in the harp trunk. Before the harp is put in the trunk, the pedals are turned *up*. When the harp is not in use, all the pedals should be placed in the flat (top) notches—leaving the instrument in the key of C♭. The harp should never be left standing in a draft, nor should it be exposed to extreme heat.

If the harp pedals are not functioning properly, the pedals may need new flannel wrappings, or the springs may need to be replaced. For repairs of any extent, or for complete over-hauling, the harp should be returned to the harp factory or the harp maker.

Tuning keys, tuning key holders (that can be attached to the harp), rubber pedal pads, tuning-pins, pegs, harp covers, etc., may be purchased individually from stores carrying harpist's supplies.

Under no circumstances should the harp be washed with soap and water, or rubbed with furniture polish. Dust the harp frequently with a soft, clean rag, and leave further cleaning (especially that which requires the removal of any parts) to be done by the experienced harp repair man. It is advisable to have the mechanism of the harp oiled—depending on the constant use of the harp. If the school instrument is used by a number of students for practice purposes, and also moved frequently from one part of the building to another, it may require minor adjustments from time to time. For this reason too, the school will want to select the most durable instrument available when purchasing a harp.

CHAPTER VIII

Some General Remarks Concerning Care of the Fingers and Fingering

A DAILY PERIOD of even, conscientious, practice is probably the best insurance against extreme and painful callouses on the finger tips. Rub the finger tips with pumice stone, or apply witch hazel, but *never* cut the callouses.

FINGERING—It is often noted, in considering the advantages of the study of the harp, that the fingering for scales remains the same in all the different keys. This is easy to understand when one considers that (for example) the string which provides the A natural for the key of C scale, is the same string which provides the necessary A*b* for the scale of the key of E*b*.

In fingering the intervals of two tones the finger placement is generally as follows (this applies to *both hands*—as the hands are playing on opposite sides of the strings, and not on the same side, as with the piano.): the interval of an octave is fingered by thumb (1) and fourth (4) finger; the interval of the seventh is fingered either by thumb and fourth finger, or by thumb and third (3) finger; the intervals of the sixth and the fifth are fingered by thumb and third finger; and the intervals of the fourth, third and second, are fingered by the thumb and the second (2) finger.

* * *

It will probably be easier for the child to comprehend the system of tetrachords, upon which our harmonic scales are based, from observation of the piano keyboard, rather than

from looking at the harp. For, once the child has identified
the strings of the harp, the first visual impression is that of
the diatonic scale in C major. (Literally, one cannot see the
"black notes").

* * *

The application of the principles of "keyboard" harmony
to the harp, would help vastly in promoting the student's
early grasp of the possibilities of the harp.

* * *

" . . . . for he who learns to play the harp learns to play
it by playing it, and all other learners do similarly."

Aristotle

Harp in the symphony orchestra—Joseph Vito, solo harpist, Chicago Symphony Orchestra, and Geraldine Vito (Mrs. John Weicher), second harpist on stage at Orchestra Hall.

Photograph by Frank C. Zak, Chicago.

PLATE XXI

Harp in the motion picture studio—Lois Adele Craft, solo harpist, 20th Century-Fox motion picture studio orchestra.

Photograph by Barnett.

Marcel Grandjany, concert and recording artist, composer; head of the harp department Juilliard School of Music.

Photograph by Victor Schertzinger.

PLATE XXIII

Harp in the radio studio—Margaret Sweeney, staff harpist of radio station
W.L.S. (Chicago); featured artist of the "Magic Harp" program.

Photograph by Bloom, Chicago.

PLATE XXIV

Harps and harp objects from the large and unique collection of Virginia Morgan (Mrs. David Robinson), first harpist, San Francisco Symphony Orchestra. Mrs. Robinson holds an interesting example of the once popular "dital-harp".

PLATE XXV

[111]

Alberto Salvi, concert and radio artist, shown informally in his private studio, with the Emperor Franz Joseph Erard harp (left) and his Wurlitzer concert harp (right).

PLATE XXVI

[112]

SECTION III

SUGGESTED MUSIC

"The harp at Nature's advent strung
Has never ceased to play;
The song the stars of morning sung
Has never died away."

WHITTIER, *The Worship of Nature*

CHAPTER I

Harp *Methods for the Beginning Student*

BOCHSA-OBERTHUR   *Universal Method*   Carl Fischer, N. Y.
            1912   150 pages $4.00

   Bochsa (1789-1856) Method for the harp, revised by Charles
Oberthur (1819-1895). Applies to both the single action and the
double action harp. Contains: rudiments of music; scales; exercises;
illustrations; 40 progressive studies; major and minor scale, and arpeggio studies; 24 preludes.

CLARK   *How to Play the Harp*   G. Schirmer, N. Y.
            1932   99 pages $2.50

   Written by Melville Clark (1883-   ) in collaboration with
the late Van Veachton Rogers. Applies to both the Irish harp and
the pedal harp. Contains: 29 illustrations; 102 exercises; 12 melodies
including English, Irish, Welsh, favorites. For "home and class study".

LAWRENCE-SALZEDO   *Method for the Harp*   G. Schirmer
            1929   71 pages $3.00

   With English and French text, by Lucile Lawrence and Carlos
Salzedo (1885-   ). Contains: exercises; technical explanations; illustrations; 15 preludes for beginners—each in a different key, to
familiarize the beginner with the manner of key formation on the
harp. This Method serves as an introduction and complement to Salzedo's MODERN STUDY OF THE HARP.

RENIE   *Methode Complete de Harpe*   Alphonse Leduc, Paris
            1946   In two volumes comprising 224 pages.

   Written by Henriette Renie in her native French, this Method
is the most comprehensive yet published. Volume I ($8.25)—Tech-
nique—includes: 12 lessons—exercises, illustrations, explanations, list·
ing of pieces to be studied in conjunction with the lessons. Volume II

THE HARP

($6.00)—includes: Syntaxe-Appendice—with difficult passages from harp parts in symphonic works. Watch for English translation—in preparation by Virginia Morgan (Robinson), to be published by Leduc, Paris.

ROBINSON   *First Lessons for the Harp*   Carl Fischer, N. Y.
63 pages $2.75

Instructions after the method of Hasselmans (1845-1912), by Gertrude Ina Robinson. Applies to both the concert harp and the small harp. Contains: rudiments—notation, scales, how to tune, time; illustrations and explanations; exercises and melodious studies.

Also Methods by:

ATTL; BAUER-ZEICH; LABARRE; OBERTHUR; SCHAEFFER-ARLING; SNOER; WOHLFAHRT; WURMSER-DELCOURT; AND ZABEL.

CHAPTER II

Albums for the Beginning Student

VERY YOUNG—Albums of little pieces:

OLD TUNES FOR YOUNG HARPISTS—Mildred Dilling

Ditson, Philadelphia
1934   48 pages

Collection of 92 familiar pieces, some with words to sing, arranged progressively; for the concert or Irish harp. Illustrated introduction to harp playing.

AN EVENING AT HOME—Alfred Holy   *Ditson, Boston*
1918   8 pages
Five easy pieces—"Children's thoughts", "At the fireside", etc.
Very melodious.

FIRST HARP BOOK—Betty Paret   *G. Schirmer, N. Y.*
1942   37 pages
Simple melodies—folk songs, etc., with words. Arranged progressively.

JUNGLE SCENES—Betty Paret   *Sprague Coleman, N. Y.*
1939   4 pages
Three easy pieces—"Little monkey swinging", "Lullaby for a baby elephant", "Giraffe argument".

TINY TALES FOR HARPIST BEGINNERS—Carlos Salzedo
Elkan-Vogel

Series I   1939   5 pages
Ten little pieces for harp or Irish harp. "Mysterious blue light", "A lost kitten", etc. Series II. 1942. 8 pages. "Winter Night", "Little Jacque's lullaby", etc.

ALBUMS FOR BEGINNING STUDENT

INTERMEDIATE—Albums of pieces and studies:

HARP ALBUM FOR BEGINNERS—Sister M. Charles
G. Schirmer
1941   27 pages
12 transcribed pieces, arranged progressively; "Study problem"
at beginning of piece.

30 LITTLE CLASSICS FOR HARP—Mildred Dilling   Ditson
1938   39 pages
Short selections from the works of Gluck, Bach, Schubert, Mozart,
Couperin, Wagner, etc.

3 EASY PIECES—Marcel Grandjany   Marks, N. Y.
1934   6 pages
Short pieces, with special attention to finger placing. "Nocturne",
"Reverie", "Barcarolle".

24 EASY STUDIES—Alfred Holy   Ditson, Boston
1918   20 pages
Arranged progressively—chords, scales, etc.

EXCERPTS AND SOLOS FOR SMALL HARP—
Gertrude Ina Robinson   C. Fischer, N. Y.
1913   29 pages
12 pieces arranged progressively, playable on the Irish or pedal
harp. "Happy Farmer" by Schumann; "Menuetto" from Mozart's
"Don Giovanni"; "Holy Night", etc.

25 LITTLE ETUDES FOR BEGINNING STUDENT—
Edmund Schuecker   C. Merseburger, Leipzig
Book I   39 pages
Etudes by Bochsa, Schuecker, Fiorillo—simple scales, chords,
octaves, etc.

POPULAR IRISH MELODIES—Gerhard Taylor
Edwin Ashdown, London
Books I, II, III   4 pages, 8 pieces per book
Simple arrangements of well known airs including: "Last Rose
of Summer", "Endearing Young Charms", etc.

CHAPTER III

Ensemble Music of Easy to Medium Grade, for the Harp with School Music Groups

ALBUM LEAF—*Wagner*, transcribed by C. E. LeMassena
  String orchestra with harp obbligato.
*AVE MARIA—*Bach-Gounod*
  Vocal or string solo with harp accompaniment.
*AVE MARIA—*Schubert*
  Vocal or string solo with harp accompaniment.
*BARCAROLLE from "Tales of Hoffman"—*Offenbach*
  Vocal solo (or chorus) with harp accompaniment.
*BERCEUSE from "Jocelyn"—*Gounod*
  Vocal solo (or chorus) with harp accompaniment.
BLUE BELLS OF SCOTLAND—Arranged by Thomas
  Voice and harp.
*CANTIQUE DE NOEL—*Adams*
  Vocal, string, or woodwind solo with harp accompaniment.
HARP OF ST. CECILIA—*Wiegane*
  Organ and harp, violin or cello, harp and organ; violin, cello
    and harp.
LARGO from "Xerxes"—*Handel*
  Violin and harp; cello and harp; two violins and harp.
MINSTREL'S CANZONET from "Yolande"—*Tschaikowsky*,
  transcribed by Quinto Maganini
  String orchestra and harp.
*ON WINGS OF SONG—*Mendelssohn*
  Vocal, string, or woodwind solo with harp accompaniment.
PROMENADE A L'AUTOMNE—*Tournier*
  Cello and harp; violin and harp.
THE ROSARY—*Nevin-Pinto*
  Harp solo with organ.
*SERENADE—*Toselli*
  Vocal or string solo with harp accompaniment.

ENSEMBLE MUSIC FOR EASY TO MEDIUM GRADE

STAR OF HOPE—*Pinto*
  Violin, cello, or flute solo with harp; violin, harp and organ trio.
STRINGS IN VARIATIONS—*Ganz,* Op. 33, No. 2
  Two violins, viola, cello, bass and harp.
*THE SWAN from "Carnival of Animals"—*Saint-Saens*
  String, or woodwind solo with harp accompaniment.

*When the arrangement or transcription for the harp is not available, the piano accompaniment may be adapted for the harp.

CHAPTER IV

Selected Composers, Compositions and Recordings

"WHO HAS COMPOSED MUSIC for the harp?", "Who has transcribed or arranged music for the harp?", and "Who has recorded music for the harp?", are questions that eventually confront all those who have interest in this instrument. In an attempt to provide at least a partial answer for these questions, the author has compiled the following list of selected composers, transcribers, arrangers and recorders of both solo and ensemble music for the harp.

Arranged in alphabetical order, this list also includes the names of composers—Bach, Mendelssohn, Chopin, etc.—who have not composed music for the harp, but whose works have been transcribed or arranged for the harp. Since some music stores are inclined to file transcribed harp music (especially albums) under the name of the *transcriber,* rather than the name of the *composer,* the names of transcribers and arrangers for the harp are listed in alphabetical order under the name of the original composers. For example:

CHOPIN, F. (1810-1849)   A
        trans Boghen, Eissler, M. Miller, Oberthur, Renie, Thomas, Vizthum.

It is hoped that such a listing will not only provide some needed clarity in ordering music, but will also give the reader some idea of the variety of transcriptions available.

The dates of birth and death, of the musicians listed, have been included whenever it was possible to obtain or determine them. Where this has not been possible, the reader may refer to the date of publication of the composer's work(s) for the harp included (either in this chapter, or in Chapters V or VI

[121]

THE HARP

of this Section), recordings, etc. for aid in determining some chronological order.

In the preceding example, the letter "A" following Chopin's name and dates, refers the reader to part "A" in Chapter V of this Section (III), where transcriptions of Chopin's works are listed.

REFERENCE ABBREVIATIONS—following the name (and dates —if available) of the composer:

V—EXTENDED USE OF THE HARP—Chapter V, Section I.
*—EVOLUTION OF THE SCHOOLS OF HARP PLAYING—Chapter V, Section I.
**—TWO EARLY VIRTUOSI—Chapter V, Section I.
VV—ORCHESTRAL USE OF THE DOUBLE ACTION HARP—Chapter V, Section I.
VI—Chapter VI—RECORDED ORCHESTRAL WORKS, Section I.
VII—Chapter VII—THE "CHROMATIC" HARP, Section I.
VIII—PROMINENT NAMES IN THE HARP WORLD PRIOR TO 1900—Chapter VIII, Section I.
VIII*—OUTSTANDING HARPISTS OF THE TWENTIES—Chapter VIII, Section I.
IX—Chapter IX—FUTURE OPPORTUNITIES, Section I.
#—AMERICAN SCHOOLS—Chapter IX, Section I.
Ix—Chapter I—HARP METHODS, ETC.—Section III.
IIx—Chapter II—ALBUMS FOR THE BEGINNING STUDENT, Section III.
IIIx—Chapter III—ENSEMBLE MUSIC, ETC., Section III.
A—SOLOS FOR SPECIAL SCHOOL PROGRAMS—Chapter V, Section III.
B—SOLO MUSIC FOR THEATRICAL PRODUCTIONS—Chapter V, Section III.
  1. Fantasy Music; 2. Incidental Music; 3. Dance Music.
C—STUDY PIECES FOR THE HARP—Chapter V, Section III.
D—PROGRAM MUSIC SOLOS—Chapter V, Section I.
VIx—Chapter VI—MUSIC FOR THE ADVANCED HARPIST, Section III.

CLASSICAL ENSEMBLE WORKS AND PHONOGRAPH RECORDINGS
Classical ensemble works of special interest, and phonograph recordings, are listed by composers. Popular music recordings

SELECTED COMPOSERS, COMPOSITIONS AND RECORDINGS

of special interest are listed under the name of the recording harpist. Names of recording harpists are given in full.

MUSIC AND RECORDING ABBREVIATIONS—appearing on the lines *below* the composer's name:

MUSIC: Album—A
        Ensemble music—Ens
        Exercises—E
        Method—M
        Music for Irish Harp—Ir
        Solo music—S
        Studies—Stu
        Transcribed by—trans (name of transcriber)
        Transcriptions for harp—trans

RECORDINGS—Reco
        Alco—AC
        (l') Anthologie Sonore—AS
        Bien—B
        Black & White—B & W
        Brunswick—Br
        Columbia—C
        Decca—D
        Decca-Odeon—D-O
        Gramaphone—G
        His Master's Voice—HMV
        Liberty—Lib
        Master—Mas
        Musicraft—Mus
        New Music Quarterly—NMQ
        Republic—Rep
        Royale—R
        Schirmer—Sch
        Victor—V
        Victrola-Orthophonic—V-O

ACHARD-PROTHIN, M.   A
    S

ADAM, A. C. (1803-1856)   IIIx
    Ens trans Pinto

ADAM, J. L. (1758-1848)
    Ens—Concertantes for harp, piano and violin (1776)

AEOLIANS—flute, viola, cello and harp
    Early Ens Reco for V

THE HARP

ALBANO, M. (1841-   )
S; trans
ALBENIZ, I. (1860-1909)   A
S; trans Bruno, Renie
ALBERSTOTTER, C.   VIII   D
S; Ens—"Ballade" for harp and orchestra, Op. 3.
ALBERTI, D.   D
S; Ens
ALETTER
Reco—"Rendezvous"—Lorenzi, harp; Torch, organ—C
148M
AMBROSE (4th century)
trans Pinto
APTOMMAS (Thomas Thomas) (1829-1913)   VIII
S; trans; E
ARDITI, L. (1822-1903)
trans Thomas
ATTL, K.   VIII*   Ix
M
BACH, J. S. (1685-1750)   III   VI   IIIx   C   VIx
trans Beon, David, Dilling, Grandjany, Kastner, Magistretti,
Oberthur, Poenitz, Renie, Salvi, Salzedo, Sister Charles,
Snoer, Tyre, Zingsem; S;   Ens;   A
Reco—"Bourree" from Partita I—Gerard, S—D 20638
—"Bourree"—Dilling, S—C
—"Gavotte" from 2nd Sonata—Bach-Saint-Saens—
Sassoli, S—4570
—"Largo" Bach-Saint-Saens-Grandjany—Grandjany, S
—V 2153
BACH, K. P. E. (1714-1788)   C
trans Gillman, M. Miller, N. S. Miller
BACHLET, A. G. (1864-   )
Ens
BACHMAN, A. (1836-   )
Ens
BACKOFEN, J. G. H. (1768-1870)
S; M; Ens
BALFE, M. (1808-1879)
trans Alberti, Dussek
BAMBRICK, W.   VIII*
S

[124]

BANTOCK, G. (1868-   )   VIx
Ens—"Coronach" for strings, harp and organ; Dramatic
Dance No. II for dancer with harp accompaniment.
BARLOW, W. (1912-   )
"Nocturne" for chamber orchestra (harp and strings)
BAUER, C. A. (1789-before 1860)
S; Ens—for flute and harp
BAUER-ZEICH, M. (1861-   )   VIII   Ix
M (1912)
BAUTISTA, J. (1901-   )
Four Galacian songs for mezzo-soprano, flute, oboe, clarinet,
viola, cello and harp.
BAX, A. (1883-   )   VIx
Ens—"Concerto" for bassoon, harp and string quartet; "Con-
certo" for flute, oboe, harp and string quartet; "In Me-
moriam" for English horn, harp and string quartet; "Irish
Elegy" for English horn, harp and strings; "Of A Rose I
Sing"—carol for small choir, harp, cello and double bass
(1921); "Quintet" for strings and harp (1919).
Reco—"Fantasy-Sonata"—Frobes, viola; Korchinka, harp—
D K941/3
—"Elegiac Trio"—Ruderman, flute; Thomas, viola;
Craft, harp—AC 205.
—"Nonet"—Griller String Quartet; Slater, bass; Wat-
son, flute; Thurston, clarinet; Goossens, oboe;
Korchinka, harp—C 386.
BAZELAIRE, P. (1886-   )   VIx
Ens—"Fantasiestuck" for harp and piano; "Suite Grecque"
for two flutes, oboe, violin, viola, two cellos, and harp
(1927).
BEDELL, R. L.   C
trans
BEDFORD, H. (1867-   )
Ens—"To A Water-lily at Evening" for voice, string quar-
tet and harp; "Nocturne" (Summer Dream) for voice,
string quartet and harp.
BEETHOVEN, L. (1770-1827)   V   B3   C
trans Bochsa, David, Dilling, Oberthur, Pinto, Poenitz,
Robinson, Sister Charles, Thomas; S; Ens
Reco—"Minuet"—Trio de Luce—C A2633
BELLINI, V. (1801-1835)
trans Oberthur, Parish-Alvars
Reco—"Norma Fantasy"—Lapitino, S—V 18119.

THE HARP

BENNET, D.
"La Rougette" for harp and concert band (1941)
BENNETT, R. R. (1894-   )
"Sonatina" for harp, flute and cello
BEON, A.   B2
S; trans; Ens
BERCKMAN, E. (1900-   )
Ens—"Archangels" suite for three harps (1932); "Incantation", "Percussion", "The Web", "Circus Day" for harp.
BEREZOWSKY, N. (1900-   )   VIx
"Concerto" for harp and orchestra (1947)
BERLIOZ, H. (1803-1869)   V   VI
"Serenade—Trio des Jeunes Ismaelites" from Oratorio
"L'Enfance du Christ", for two flutes and harp.
Reco—Moyse, Manouvrier, flutes; Laskine, harp—D 25750
BERMAN, RUTH
Reco—"String Time"—harp and orchestra—popular songs
—Lib (album)
BERNARD, J. E. (1843-1902)
Reco—"Ca fait peur aux oiseaux"—Marquet, soprano and
Laskine, harp—G—DA 4836.
BERNHEIM, M.   D
S
BISHOP, H. R. (1786-1855)
Reco—"Home Sweet Home"—Salvi, S—V-O 4001.
BIZET, G. (1838-1875)   VI
trans Delsaux, Verdalle, Wetsger; Ens—"Menuetto" from
"Arlesienne Suite No. II"—for flute, harp and orchestra.
Reco—See Section I, Chapter VI.
BLACK, N. B.   A   D
trans; S
BLISS, A. (1891-   )   VIx
"Madame Noy" for soprano, flute, clarinet, bassoon, viola,
harp and double bass (1918).
BLUMENTHAL, J. (1827-1908)   D
trans Chatterton, Hasselmans, Thomas.
BOCHSA, R. N. C. (1789-1856)   *   **   Ix
Numerous S; Stu; M; E
BOISDEFFRE, R. DE (1838-1906)   A
trans J. Vito

[126]

SELECTED COMPOSERS, COMPOSITIONS AND RECORDINGS

BONNER, E. M. (1889-   )
Four songs for medium voice, flute, clarinet, bassoon and harp, Op. 10.
"La Chanson du Porc-epic", "La Complainte de M. Benoit", "Chameaux", "Paysage de Neige".

BRAGA, G. (1829-1907)
trans Hasselmans, Oberthur, J. Vito.

BRAHMS, J. (1833-1897)   VV   B2   D   VIx
trans Fels, N. S. Miller, Salzedo; Ens—Four songs for chorus, French horn and harp.

BRANSCOMBE, G. (1881-   )
"Across the Blue Aegean Sea" for soprano, harp, flute, two clarinets, and French horn (1939).

BRITAIN, R. (1904-   )
S

BRITTAIN, A.   A   B1
S

BRITTEN, B. (1913-   )
"A Ceremony of Carols" for women's chorus, soprano soli, and two harps.

BULL, J. (1562-1628)
trans Grandjany.
Reco—"King's Hunt"—Grandjany, S—V 2095.

BUSSER, H. P. (1872-   )
S; Ens—"Piece de Concert" for harp and small orchestra, Op. 32; "Impromptu on Japanese Tunes" for chromatic harp and orchestra, Op. 58; "Ballade in A♭ Major" for harp and strings (1918).
Reco—"Piece de Concert"—Laskine, harp and orchestra, Prüwer, conducting—G—L 1031.

CADMAN, C. W. (1881-1946)   D
trans Z. Clark, Keller.

CADY, H.
Reco—"Danse Oriental"—Dilling, S—C 17069.

CAMERON, W. T.   A   D
S

CAPLET, A. (1878-1925)   VIx
S; Ens—"Conte Fantastique" after Edgar Allan Poe—for harp and strings; "Le Miroir de Jesus" for string quintet, harp, three female voices (1923).

THE HARP

CARAMIELLO, S. (1831-before 1920)
S; trans
CARDON, L. (1747-1805)
M (1805).
CARUSI, I.   VIII
trans
CELLA, T.   VIII*   B1   B3
S; Ens; Ir S
CHABRIER, A. (1841-1894)
S
CHALLONER, N. B. (1784-after 1829)
S; Ens; M (1806)
CHALMERS, H.   B1   B2   B3   C   D
Numerous S; Ens
CHAPUIS, A. P. (1862-   )
S
CHARPENTIER, G. (1860-   )
Ens—voice and harp
CHATTERTON, F. (1795-before 1880)
S; trans
CHATTERTON, J. B. (1805-1871)   *   A
S; trans; Ens—voice and harp
CHERTOK, PEARL
Reco—"Around the Clock"—original suite for harp—
"Ten Past Two", "Beige Nocturne", "Harpicide at Mid-
night", "The Morning After"—Rep PC 101/2.
CHESHIRE, J. (1839-1910)   VIII   A   B1   D
Numerous S; trans Ens
CHIPP, P. T. (1793-1849)
S
CHOPIN, F. (1810-1849)   A
trans Boghen, Eissler, M. Miller, Oberthur, Renie, Thomas,
Vizthum.
Reco—"Fantasy Impromptu"—Salvi, S—V 55141.
CIALONE, V. (1869-   )
S; Ens—duets
CIMAROSA, D. (1749-1801)
trans Pinto
CLARK, M. A. (1883-   )   IV   IX
Two M (1919, 1923)
CLARK(E), Z.   VIII*   D
trans

SELECTED COMPOSERS, COMPOSITIONS AND RECORDINGS

CLEMENTI, M. (1752-1832)
    trans Salvi
CLINTON, J. (1810-1864)
    Ens—duets for flute and harp
COCKERILL, JOHN   *
    Early Ens Reco for V
COERNE, L. A. (1870-1922)
    "Concerto in E" for strings, organ, harp and horn, Op. 12,
    (1892).
COEUR, V.   B3   D
    Ens; A; trans
CORELLI, A. (1653-1713)   C
    trans Pinto, Salzedo
COUPERIN, F. (1668-1733)   C
    trans Dilling, Grandjany, Renie, Salzedo
    Reco—"La Commère"—Renie, S—D 20518.
       —"Soeur Monique"—Grandjany, S—V 12-0171 (al-
         bum V DM1201).
       —"Tic toc choc"—Dilling, S—C
CRAFT, LOIS ADELE
    Reco—Classical Ens (see Bax)
CRAS, J. (1879-1932)
    "Quintet" for harp and strings (April 1928)
CRESTON, P. (1906-   )
    "Poem" for harp and orchestra
CZERNY, K. (1791-1877)
    Stu trans Caramiello, Vizthum
DALVIMARE, M. P. (1772-1808)
    S; Ens—duets
DANDRIEU, J. F. (1684-1740)
    trans Renie
DANIELS, M. W. (1879-   )
    "Songs of Elfland" for soprano soli, women's voices, flute,
    harp, strings and percussion (1924).
DAQUIN, L. C. (1694-1772)   C
    trans Magistretti, Renie
    Reco—"L'Hirondelle"—Renie, S—D 20517.
DARNTON, C. (1891-   )
    Ens—"Concerto" for harp and winds (1935) ; "Suite" for
    flute, viola and harp (1935).
DAVID, A. L. (1881-   )   A   B1   B3   D
    A—two volumes (1916)

[129]

THE HARP

DEBUSSY, C. (1863-1918)   B3   C   D   VV   VI
VII   VIx
   S trans Coeur, Grandjany, Jacquet, Lautermann, Renie.
   Reco—"Arabesque No. I"—Cockerill, S—C DX1311 (Ravel
       album) ; Dilling, S—G C1642; Sassoli, S—V
    —"En Bateau"—Reardon, S—Sch 5507.
    —"Maid with the Flaxen Hair"—Newell, S—C 70083.
   Ens—"Children's Corner" trans Salzedo
   Reco—Barrere, flute; Britt, cello; Salzedo, harp—V V639.
   "Dances—Sacred and Profane" for harp and orchestra
   Reco—Grandjany, harp; Victor String Orchestra, Levin
       conducting—V DM1021.
    —Jamet, harp; instrumental accompaniment—G W1562.
    —Laskine, harp; orchestra, Coppola conducting—G
       W1025.
    —Phillips, harp; Philadelphia Orchestra, Stokowski
       conducting—V 7455 (album V 116).
   "Sonata No. II" for flute, viola and harp
   Reco—Moyse, Ginto, Laskine—D 20085/7.
    —Moyse, Merckel, Laskine—V M873.
    —Tassinari, Mora, Gandolfi—C CQX16491/2.
    —Wummer, Katims, Newell—C X-282.
DEGRANDVAL, C. (1830-1907)   VIx
   Ens—flute and harp
DELIBES, L. (1836-1891)
   trans Fel, Renie
DELLO JOIO, N.
   "Concerto" for harp and orchestra (premiere 1947)
DESEVERAC, D. (1873-1921)
   Reco—"An Old Music Box"—Dilling, S—C 17073.
    —"Le Roi a Fait Battre"—Marquet, soprano; Laskine,
       harp—G DA4836.
DESTENAY, E.
   Ens—"Conte de Vielle" for harp and orchestra, Op. 30;
   "Quintet in Eb" for two violins, viola, cello and harp,
   Op. 12, (1905).
DIENEL, O. (1839-1905)
   Ens
DILLING, MILDRED   IIx
   Two A; trans Numerous S Reco for C and G (see Bach.
   Cady, Couperin, Debussy, DeServac, Hasselmans, Poenitz.
   Prokofieff, Sibelius, Tournier).

[130]

Reco—"March of the Men of Harlech" (Welsh air) ; "Believe Me If All Those Endearing Young Charms"—S— C 17065.

D'INDY, V. (1851-1931)
"Suite" for flute, violin, viola, cello and harp, Op. 91 (1930)
Entrée, En sonate, Air desuet, Sarabande, Farandole.
Reco—Paris Instrumental Quintet (Laskine, harp)—V 11668/9.

DISTEFANO, STE. A B2
S; Ens; trans

DIZI, F. (1789-1840) *
Numerous S; Sonatas—revised by Posse; Stu—revised by Hasselmans; M (1827).

DOLMETSCH, A. (1858-1940)
trans Hasselmans

DONIZETTI, G. (1797-1848) C D
trans Bochsa, Chatterton, David, Labarre, Oberthur, Parish-Alvars, Salzedo, Schuecker, Wright, Zabel.
Reco—"Lucia Prelude"—Lapitino, S—V 18119.

DONOVAN, R. F. (1891-)
"Wood-notes" for flute, harp and string orchestra (1925).

DRDLA, F. (1868-)
trans Pinto

DRESDEN, S. (1881-)
"Sonata" for flute and harp (1918)

DUBEZ, J. D
S
Reco—"Songs Without Words"—Schuetze, S—C A968.

DUBOIS, T. (1837-1924) D
trans Delcourt, Renie; Ens—"Fantasie" for harp and orchestra.

DUPHLY C
trans Renie

DUPIN, P. (1865-)
First of "Pieces Dialogues" for flute, cello and harp

DUPONT, A. (1828-1890)
Ens

DURAND, A. C
trans Hasselmans, Pinto, Renie, Salzedo

DURANTE, F. (1684-1755)
trans Pinto

DUSSEK, J. L. (1761-1812) B3
S; Ens—Concertos, sonatas, trios

[131]

THE HARP

DUSSEK, MME. S. (1774-1847)
    S
DVORAK, A. (1841-1904)   A   D
    trans Lapitino, Pinto, Robinson, Salzedo, Zunova
    Reco—"Humoresque"—Lapitino, S—V 18119.
EGAN, C.
    M (1829)
EICHHEIM, H. (1878-   )
    "Oriental Impressions" for piano, harp, violins, flute, oboe,
    cor anglaise, bells and percussion.
ELGAR, E. (1857-1934)
    trans Pinto
ELOUIS, J. (active during 1790-1812)
    Numerous S
FABIANI, H. B.   VIII
    S; Stu
FALLA, M. DE (1876-1946)   VIx
    trans Grandjany; Ens—"Psyche" for mezzo-soprano, flute,
    harp, oboe, clarinet, violin and cello (1924) ; "A Cordoba"
    for voice and harp (1927).
FARNABY, G. (1560-1600)   VIx
    Ens trans Hill
FAURE, G. (1845-1924)   VV   A   B1   VIx
    trans Delsart, Grandjany, Hasselmans, Kahn
    Reco—"Impromptu for Harp"—Laskine, S—V 12005.
FERRARI, G. G. (1759-1842)
    Ens
FERRO, P.
    "Suite agreste" for flute, English horn, clarinet, viola, harp
    and voice (1923).
FEVRIER, H. (1876-   )
    S
FLEURY, L. (1878-1926)
    Ens—flute and harp
FLORENTINE QUARTET—violin, flute, cello and harp
    Early Ens Reco for V
FLOTOW, F. VON (1812-1883)
    trans Alberti, Oberthur, Salvi, Salzedo
    Reco—"Last Rose of Summer" from "Martha"—Salvi,
    S—V 45315
FORST, R. (1900-   )   D
    S; Ens—trio

FOSTER, S. (1826-1864)   D
  trans Lapitino, Riley (album), Salvi, Salzedo
  Reco—"Old Folks at Home"—Salvi, S—V-O 4001.
FRANCISQUE, A. (1570-1605)
  trans Grandjany
  Reco—"Pavane and Bransles"—Grandjany, S—V 12-0170
      (album V DM1201)
FREED, I. (1900-   )
  S; Ens—trio for flute, harp and viola.
FRESCOBALDI, G. (1583-1643)
  trans Pinto
FRIED, O. (1871-   )
  Piece for thirteen winds, two harps and drums.
FRIML, R. (1881-   )
  trans Eagle, E. Vito
GALLON, N. (1891-   )   VIx
  S
GALUPPI, B. (1706-1785)
  trans Magistretti
GANDOLFI, CELESTE
  Early S and Ens Reco for C (see Debussy, Tedeschi)
GANNE, L. G. (1862-1923)
  Ens
GANZ, R. (1877-   )   IIIx
  Ens
GASSMAN, F. (1723-1774)
  S
GASSMAN, R.
  Ens—"Brave New World" cantata for baritone, clarinet,
      cello, harp and piano (1947).
GATAYES, G. P. A. (1774-1846)
  S; M; Ens—duets
GATAYES, J. L. (1805-1884)
  S
GAUBERT, P. (1879-   )
  "Divertissement Grec" for two flutes and harp; S
GERARD, GENEVIEVE
  Reco—S for D (see Bach, Hasselmans)
GILLIS, D.
  "Rhapsody" for harp and orchestra (premiere 1947)
GILSON, P. (1865-   )
  S

THE HARP

GLIERE, R. M. (1875-   )
"Concerto" for harp and orchestra (1938)
GLUCK, C. W. (1714-1787)   VI   B3
trans Dilling, Maneke, Salzedo, Snoer
GODARD, B. (1849-1895)
trans Hasselmans, Pinto; Ens
GODEFROID, F. (1818-1897)   *   A   B1   VI
Numerous S; Stu; A; trans Grandjany
Reco—"Etude de Concert"—Grandjany, S—V 2117.
GODOWSKY, L. (1870-   )
trans Salvi
GOLESTAN, S. (1876-   )
Reco—"Ballade Roumaine"—Laskine, S—G L985.
    —"Intermezzo et Sicilienne"—Laskine, harp and Cham-
        ber Orchestra, Oubradous conducting—
        G DB11157.
GONDOLIER TRIO—violin, flute and harp
Early Ens Reco for Br
GOOSSENS, E. (1893-   )   VIx
S; Ens—"Suite" for violin, flute and harp, Op. 6 (1918)
GOOSSENS, SIDONIE
Reco—"Londonderry Air"—Primrose, viola; Goossens, harp
    —C 7378M.
GOTTHELF, F. (1857-1930)
"Hymnus" for violin, cello, harp and organ.
GOULD, M. (1913-   )
"Harvest" for strings, harp and vibraphone.
GOUNOD, C. (1818-1893)   IIIx
Ens; trans Lebano, Oberthur, Thomas, Verdalle
GRAENER, P. (1873-   )
"Symphonietta für Streichinstrumente und Harfe" (1910).
GRANADOS, E. (1867-1916)
trans Bruno, Salvi
GRANDJANY, MARCEL (1891-   )   III   IX   #   A
B2   B3   C   D   IIx   VIx
Numerous S; A; Classical trans; trans; Ens—"Poeme Sym-
    phonique" for harp, horn and orchestra; harp duos; harp
    trios; Numerous Reco—original compositions and trans
    for V (see Bach, Bull, Couperin, Debussy, Francisque,
    Handel, Kirchhoff, Loeillet, Ravel).
Reco—"Automne"—S—V 10-1120.
    —"Rhapsodie"—S—V 2060.

—Two popular French songs—"Le Bon Petit Roi d'Yvette", and "Et Ron Ron Ron Petit Patapon"— S—V 2095; Dilling, S—C 17073.

GRETCHANINOFF, A. (1864-   ) VIx
trans Grandjany; Ens—flute and harp; voice, cello and harp.
Reco—"Allegro vivace"—Grandjany, S—V 10-1120.

GRIEG, E. (1843-1907)
trans Carusi, Pinto, J. Vito.

GROVLEZ, G. (1879-   )
S

GRUBER, F. X. (1787-1863)
trans Grandjany, Joseph, Robinson, Salzedo, J. Vito

GUERRINI, G. (1890-   )
S

HAHN, A.   D
S

HALLE, A. DE LA (1238-1288)
Reco—Early French songs—Dixon, tenor, accompanied by lute and harp—V 20227.

HANDEL, G. F. (1685-1759)   III   A   D   IIIx
VIx
trans Bedell, Beon, Dilling, DiStefano, Grandjany, Helmsberger, Hunter, Magistretti, Martenot, Pampari, Reinhard, Salzedo, Snoer, Stern, Thomas, Wellman, Zellner.
Ens—"Concerto in Bb"—trans for harp alone, with original cadenza by Grandjany (1933); Cadenza by Salzedo (1947).
Reco—Laskine, harp; Orchestra, Rosenthal conducting— D 20174/5.
—Grandjany, harp; Victor Chamber Orchestra, Morel conducting—V DM1201.

HANSON, H. (1896-   )
Ens—"Concerto" for organ, strings and harp; "Serenade" for flute, harp and strings (1940).

HARRISON, J. (1885-   )
"Prelude music" for two violins, viola, cello and harp (1912).

HARTY, H. H. (1879-1941)
S

HASS, A.   A
trans

[135]

THE HARP

HASSELMANS, A. (1845-1912)   *   VIII   A   B1
B2   B3   C   D
   Numerous S; Ens; trans Stu Bochsa, Dizi, Heller, Labarre,
   Lavrier, Naderman
   Reco—"Follets"—Laskine, S—V 4438
     —"Prayer"—Sassoli, S—V 70027
     —"Patrouille" (petit marche characteristique)—Laskine,
     S—V 4438
     —"La Source"—Gerard, S—D 20368; Dilling, S—C
     17069.
     —"Valse de Concert"—Sassoli, S—V 70088

HAUSSERMANN, J. (1909-   )
   "Pastoral Fantasy" for flute, harp and strings, Op. 5 (1939).

HAYDN, J. (1732-1809)   III
   trans Dilling, Renie, Salzedo; Ens—"Sonata" for harp with
   flute and bass.

HECHT, E. (1832-1887)
   Ens

HELLER, S. (1815-1888)
   Stu trans Hasselmans

HIER, E. G. (1889-   )
   "Suite" for voice, flute, viola, cello and harp.

HILL, M. W. (contemporary American composer)   VIx
   Ens trans

HINDEMITH, P. (1895-   )   VIx
   S; Ens—Concert music for piano, harp and brass, Op. 49;
   "Concerto" for flute, oboe, clarinet, bassoon, harp and
   orchestra (premiere May 1949); "The Harp that Once
   Through Tara's Halls" for mixed chorus, piano or harp,
   strings (1941).

HOBERG, M.   A
   S; Ens

HOCHBRUCKER, C. (1733-   )
   S; Ens—duets, airs

HOLY, A. (1866-1948)   VIII*   *   II   B1
   S; Stu; A; Ens

HORN, H. (1789-before 1870)
   S; M

HUBER, W. (1874-   )
   S; Ens—"Fantasie" for harp and orchestra, Op. 9, (1899).

HUMMEL, F. (1855-1928)
S; Ens—"Grand Concert Fantasy in A♭ Minor" for harp and orchestra, Op. 30; "Nocturne" for cello, harp and harmonium.

HUNTER, L. G.   D
trans

IBERT, J. (1890-   )   D
S; Ens—Trio for violin, harp and cello.

INGENHOVEN, J. (1876-   )
"Piece" for flute, clarinet and harp (1920).

INGHELBRECHT, D. E. (1880-   )   VIx
Ens—"Quintette in C Minor" for harp and string quartet, (1917); "Sonata" for flute and harp, (1918).

IPPOLITOFF-IVANOFF, M. M. (1857-1935)
"An Evening in Georgia" for flute, oboe, clarinet, bassoon and harp, Op. 69a.

JACOBI, F. (1891-   )
"Rhapsodie" for strings and harp (1940).

JAMET, PIERRE
trans; Reco—Classical music (see Debussy, Mozart)
Reco—"Indian Melodies of Peru"—Vallin, soprano; LeRoy, flute; Jamet, harp—C P4219, 4220.

JONES, E. (1752-1824)
S (Welsh airs); A

JONGEN, J. (1873-   )   VIx
Ens—"Concert A Cinq" for flute, violin, viola, cello and harp, Op. 71; "Suite de Pieces" for flute, harp, and cello, Op. 80; "Danse Lente" for flute and harp.

JUNGMANN, A. (1824-1892)
"Will-o'-the-Wisp" for harp and string orchestra, Op. 217, No. 3.

KASTNER, A. (1870-1948)   VIII*   *   #   B2
S; E; Orchestral Stu

KEMPTER, L. (1844-1919)
Ens

KIENZL, W. (1857-   )
Ens

KIRCHHOFF, G. (1685-1746)
trans Grandjany
Reco—"Aria and Rigaudon"—Grandjany, S—12-0172 (album V DM1201)

KJERULF, H. (1815-1868)
trans Pinto

THE HARP

KLEEMAN, H. (1863-   )
S
KLICKA, J. (1855-   )
Numerous S
KLUGHARDT, A. (1847-1902)
Ens; trans Holy
KOECHLIN, C. (1867-   )
S for chromatic harp
KORCHINKA, MARIE
Reco—with Ens for C, D (see Bax)
KORMAN, H. L.
"Das hohe Lied" for harp, violin and cello (1923).
KOSTELANETZ, A. (contemporary American conductor and composer)
S
KRUMPHOLZ, J. B. (1745-1790)   *
S; Ens—for harp and orchestra, quartets, etc.
LABARRE, T. (1805-1870)   *
Numerous S; M; Ens—duets, trios, etc.
LACHNER, F. (1804-1890)
Ens—concertos for harp and bassoon, trios.
LAJTHA, L.
"Trio" for harp, flute and cello Op. 22 (1937).
LAPITINO, FRANCIS
S; trans; Reco—S and Ens for V (see Bellini, Donizetti, Dvorak, Mendelssohn, Thomas).
Reco—"Christmas Hymns" S—V 19822; "Fireside Music Box", S—V 22403.
LASKINE, LILY   *
trans; Numerous Reco for G, D and V (see Berlioz, Debussy, D'Indy, Faure, Handel, Hasselmans, Mozart, Nadermann, Pierne, Ravel).
LASSEN, E. (1830-1904)
S
LAUBER, J. (1864-   )   VIx
Ens—flute and harp
LAWRENCE, LUCILE   VIII*   Ix   B1   VIx
M (with Salzedo); trans; "Art of Modulation" (with Salzedo). Reco (see Salzedo).
LEBANO, F. (1857-1919)   VIII
S
LECUONA, E. (contemporary Cuban pianist and composer)   VIx
trans Grandjany

[138]

SELECTED COMPOSERS, COMPOSITIONS AND RECORDINGS

LEONARDO, J.   C   D
S

LEONCAVALLO, R. (1858-1919)
trans Verdalle

LIADOF, A. (1855-1914)
"Tabatiére a Musique" for flauto piccolo, two flutes, three
clarinets, harp and bells, Op. 32; trans Renie.

LIEURENCE, T. (1878-   )   D
trans Macquarrie

LISZT, F. (1811-1886)   VV   VI   D
trans Black, Maxwell, Pflughaupt, Posse, Renie, Schuecker;
Ens—"Hymne de L'Enfant a Son Reveil" for female chorus,
orchestra and harp; "St. Cecilia" for mezzo-soprano,
chorus, piano, harp and harmonium.

LOEFFLER, C. M. (1861-1935)
"Psalm CXXVII—By the Rivers of Babylon" for four part
chorus of women's voices with accompaniment of organ,
harp, two flutes, cello obbligato, (1907).

LOEILLET, J. B. (1653-1728)   C
trans Grandjany
Reco—"Toccata"—Grandjany, S—V 2153.

LORENZ, J. H. (1862-1924)
S

LORENZI, MARIO
Reco—with organ for C (see Aletter, Saint-Saens)

LOUISE, ANITA (motion picture actress).
Reco—"Anita Louise at the Harp" assisted by Thaulow,
violin and Tonhazy, cello—R album No. 30.

LOUKINE, W.   A   B1   B2   C   D
S

LUBIN, E. V. (1916-   )
"Concertino" for flute, harp, celeste and strings, Op. 13
(1923).

LULLY, J. B. (1632-1687)
trans Grandjany, Renie

MACDOWELL, E. (1861-1908)
trans Salvi

MACQUARRIE, M.   A   D
trans

MAGNINI, Q. (1897-   )   III
Ens trans

[139]

MAGISTRETTI, L. M.
E (1918) ; trans; Classical trans
MALIPIERO, G. F. (1882-   )
"Sonata a Cinque" for flute, violin, viola, cello and harp
(first performance 1925).
MARCUCCI, F. (1800-1871)
S; Stu
MARIN, M. DE (1769-1830)   **
S; Ens—"Quintet" for strings and harp, Op. 14; "Duet"
for violin and harp, Op. 17.
MARTIN, F. (1890-   )   VIx
"Symphony Concertante" for harp, harpsichord, piano and
two string orchestras (American premiere 1948).
MARTINI, P. G. (1706-1784)
trans Salzedo
MASCAGNI, P. (1863-1945)
trans Robinson
MASON, D. G. (1873-   )   VIx
"Suite" for flute, harp and string quartet, (1923)
Sarabande, Elegy, Caprice
Reco—Eddy Brown Ensemble—R 1867/8.
MASON, MISS G.
Early Ens Reco for C (see Ravel).
MASON, L. (1792-1872)
trans Robinson
MASSENET, J. (1842-1912)
trans Marsick, N. S. Miller, Verdalle
MATHAIS, G. A. (1862-1910)
S
MAXWELL, ROBERT   VIx
S (popular) ; Reco
Reco—"Harpist's Holiday"—popular music—C 149
(album).
McCOLLIN, F. (1892-   )
"How Living are the Dead" for mixed chorus, harp and
organ (1941).
McDONALD, H. (1899-   )   VIx
"Suite—From Childhood" for harp and orchestra, (1941)
Reco—Phillips, harp and Philadelphia Orchestra, Ormandy
conducting—V M839 (album).
MENDELSSOHN, F. (1809-1847)   A   D
trans Cheshire, Coeur, Dilling, Hasselmans, Hunter, Lapitino,
N. S. Miller, Oberthur, Salzedo, Zamara.

Reco—"Consolation"—Lapitino, S—V 18119.
　—"Spring Song"—Trio de Luce, Ens—C A2633.
MEYER, P. (1737-1819)
　S; E; M
MIGOT, C. (contemporary French composer)
　"Quartet" for flute, clarinet, violin and harp.
MIGOT, G. (1891-　　)
　Ens—"Suite de Concert" for voice, harp, celeste, cymbals, and
　　double bass; "Concert" for flute, cello and harp; "Trio"
　　for flute, clarinet and harp; S.
MILLER, M.　C　D
　trans
MILLER, N. S.　A　B3　C　D
　S; trans
MILLS, VERLYE　B1
　A (1943) ; Reco—popular music, for V
　Reco—"Dick Liebert at the Organ" accompanied by: Mills,
　　harp, E. Vito, harp; bass; drums; guitar; oboe;
　　clarinet; English horn—popular songs—V P164.
MOLIQUE, W. B. (1802-1869)
　trans Clinton, Oberthur.
MORGAN, M. (1864-　　)
　S; Ens trans for church music.
MOSSOLOV, A. (1900-　　)
　"Concerto" for harp and orchestra (1939 Moscow Festival).
MOSTLER, N. M. (1839-1881)
　trans Scaradsche
MOZART, W. A. (1756-1791)　III　B3　C　VIx
　trans Chatterton, Dilling, Gillman, Oberthur, Renie, Robin-
　son, Schaeffer, Snoer, Streatter.
　Ens—"Concerto in C Major" for flute, harp and orchestra
　　(1778) K 299. (Cadenzas by: Cramer, Reinecke, Thomas).
　Reco—Crunelle, flute; Jamet, harp; orchestra conducted by
　　Cloez—AS—122/5 (Vol. XIII).
　　—Moyse, flute; Laskine, harp; orchestra, Coppola con-
　　　ducting—HMV—7219-7221 (album).
　　—Moyse, flute; Laskine, harp; orchestra, Coppola con-
　　　ducting—V 141.
　　—First movement only—Lemmone, flute; Sassoli, harp
　　　—V 70029.
MUSSORGSKI, M. P. (1839-1881)
　trans Ssaradgeff (1931)

NADERMANN, F. J. (1773-1835)   *
> S; Ens; Stu (revised by Hasselmans-Martenot, Schuecker, Zamara).
> Reco—"Rondo"—Laskine, S—D 20175.

NAVONE, G.   B2
> S

NEAPOLITAN TRIO—violin, flute and harp.
> Early Ens Reco for V

NEVIN, E. (1862-1901)   IIIx
> trans Pinto, Salvi
> Reco—"Mighty lak' a Rose"—Salvi, S—V 45315.

NEWELL, LAURA
> Reco—Classical music (see Debussy, Ravel, Schumann) ;
>> Popular music with "New Friends of Rhythm" for V.
> Reco—"The Minstrel Boy"—Lynch, tenor; Wummer, flute; Newell, harp; Rose, cello—C 722.

NICOLETTA, F. A.   VIIIx   B3
> S; Ir S

NIELSON, L. (1876-   )
> "Schlummert sanft in heil'ger Ruh" for voice, strings and harp, Op. 23.

NORDEN, N. L. (1887-   )
> Ens

OBERTHUR, C. (1819-1895)   *   I   B1   B2   D
VI
> Numerous S; M; E; Ens—"Concertino" for harp and orchestra, Op. 175; "Loreley" legend for orchestra with harp obbligato, Op. 108; "Trio" for violin, harp and cello, Op. 139.

O'CAROLAN, T. (1670-1738)
> Numerous S

OEHLSCHEGEL, A. (1847-before 1940)
> Ens

OFFENBACH, J. (1819-1880)   IIIx
> trans Salzedo, Seydel, Verdalle

PALESTRINA (1525-1594)
> trans Pinto

PALMGREN, S. (1878-   )
> trans Wightman

PARADISI, P. D. (1710-1792)
> trans Magistretti, Renie

[142]

PARET, B.   IIx   A   D
  Stu (1942) ; S; trans
PARISH-ALVARS, E.   (1808-1849)   *   VIx
  Numerous S; Ens—Concertos for harp and orchestra, duets;
    Numerous trans
  Reco—"Fantasie in B♭"—Salvi, S—V 55141.
PARKHURST, H. E.   (1848-1916)   D
  S; Ens
PARRY, J.   (1776-1851)
  S
PARRY, J. 0.   (1810-1879)
  S
PERGOLESI, G.   (1710-1736)
  trans Pinto
PERRACHIO, L.   VIx
  S (1928)
PESCETTI, G. B.   (1704-1766)   C
  trans Salzedo
PESSARD, E. L. F.   (1843-1917)
  S; S for chromatic harp.
PETRINI, F.   (1744-1819)
  S; M; Ens
PHILLIPS, EDNA   #
  Reco—for C and V (see Debussy, McDonald, White)
PIERNE, G.   (1863-1937)   VIx
  S; trans Hasselmans; Ens—"Variations Libres et Finales",
    quintet for flute, violin, viola, cello and harp.
  Reco—"Concertpiece"—Laskine, harp; Pasdeloup orchestra,
      Coppola conducting—G K 7621/2.
    —"Impromptu Caprice"—Laskine, S—G L985.
PIERNE, P.   (1874-   )
  Ens
PINTO, A. FRANCIS (-1948)   VIII*   A   B2   C
  D
  Numerous S; Numerous trans; A; Ir S; Ens—"Irish Rhap-
    sody No. I" for harp and orchestra (1917). Early Ens
    Reco for C.
PLANCHETT, D. C.   (1857-before 1935)
  S
POËNITZ, F.   (1850-1913)   VIII   A
  S; trans; Ens—"Vineta" fantasy for orchestra with harp
    obbligato, Op. 74, (1907).
  Reco—"Old Music Box"—Dilling, S—C 17073.

THE HARP

Ponce, M. (1885-   )
   trans Black, J. Vito
Posse, W. (1852-1926)   *   VIII   B1   B3   C
   D
   S; Stu; A; Ens; trans
Presle, J. DE LA (contemporary French composer)
   S
Prokofieff, S. (1891-   )
   S
   Reco—"Prelude in C" Op. 12#7—Dilling, S—C 17107;
      Renie, S—D 20518.
Prumier, A. (1794-1868)
   Numerous S; Ens
Prumier, A. C. (1820-1884)
   S; Stu; Ens
Pugnani, G. (1731-1798)
   trans Pinto
Rameau, J. P. (1683-1764)   A   C
   trans Caramiello, Grandjany, Renie, Salzedo
   Reco—"La Pantomine", "La Timide", "L'Indiscrete"— Bar-
      rere, flute; Britt, cello; Salzedo, harp—V 1975.
   —"La Cupis", "Tambourins"—Barrere, flute; Britt,
      cello; Salzedo, harp—V 1976.
Rapaport, E. (1900-   )
   Ens—"Israfel" for flute, harp and string orchestra (1936);
   "Quartet" for violin, cello, clarinet and harp (1935).
Rasch, H. A. (1873-   )
   Ens
Ravel, M. (1857-1937)   VI   VIx
   Ens—"Pavane"—harp part trans Lawrence; "Introduction
      and Allegro" for harp, flute, clarinet and string quartet
      (1906).
   Reco—"Introduction and Allegro"
      —Cockerill, Murchie, Draper, Virtuoso String Quartet
         —V 9738.
      —Grandjany, Victor Chamber Orchestra—V DM1020.
      —Laskine, Moyse, Delecluse, Calvert Quartet—V 4509.
      —Mason, Murchie, Draper, Woodhouse, Dinsey, Tom-
         linson, James, with Ravel conducting—C 60791/2.
      —Newell, Wummer, McLane, Stuyvesant Quartet—CM
         X167.

SELECTED COMPOSERS, COMPOSITIONS AND RECORDINGS

READ, G. (1913-   )
 S; Ens—"Poem" for solo horn in F, or viola, harp and
  strings, with violin solo.

REARDON, CASPER (1907-1941)
 Reco—Classical music for Sch (see Debussy, Salzedo,
  Suesse); Popular music with orchestra for Sch Library.

REBIKOFF, V. (1866-1920)
 Ens

REED, SUSAN
 Reco—"Folk Songs and Ballads" arranged by Susan Reed,
  sung to accompaniment of Irish harp and zither—
  V M1986 and V M1107.

REICHARDT, J. F. (1752-1814)
 trans Robinson

REINECKE, C. (1824-1910)   VIx
 "Concerto in E Minor" for harp and orchestra, Op. 182
  (1884).

RENIE, HENRIETTE (1875-   )   *   A   B3   C
 D   Ix   VIx
 Numerous S; Classical trans; trans; Several A; Numerous
  Reco for D (see Couperin, Daquin, Prokofieff, Schubert,
  Zabel); M in two volumes (1946); Ens—"Elegy" for
  harp and orchestra; "Caprice" for harp and orchestra.
 Reco—"Concerto in C Minor"—Renie, harp; Paris Phil-
  harmonic Orchestra, Cloez conducting—First two
  movements—D-O 25407/8.
  —"Contemplation"—S—D-O 25050.
  —"Legende"—S—D-O 25549.

RESPIGHI, O. (1879-1936)
 trans Grandjany, Renie
 Reco—"Siciliana"—Renie, S—D 20517; Grandjany, S—V
  2117.

RIEGGER, W. (1885-   )
 "Divertissement" for flute, harp and cello (1933)
 Reco—"Finale" from trio—Barrere, flute; Salzedo, harp;
  Britt, cello—NMQ 1012.

RILEY, J.   D
 A (1940)

RIMSKY-KORSAKOV, N. (1844-1908)   VV   VI
 Ens trans Pinto

RIVERIA TRIO—violin, harp and cello.
 Early Ens Reco for Br

ROBERTS, E. (1819-1873)
M for Welsh triple harp
ROBINSON, G. I.   *   VIII*   B1   B2   B3   D
   Ix   IIx
   S; Stu; Ir A; trans; Ens
ROCCA, L. (1895-   )
   Ens
ROGER-DUCASSE, J. J. (1873-   )   B2
   S; Ens—"Variations Plaisantes sur un Theme Grave" for
   harp and orchestra (1907).
ROGERS, V. V. (1864-now deceased)   VIII   A   B1
   B3   D
   Numerous S; Ir S; Ens; A
ROHOZINSKI, L. (contemporary Polish composer)
   "Suite Breve" for flute, viola and harp (1923)
ROLLE, J. H. (1718-1785)
   trans Magistretti
ROPARTZ, J. G. (1864-   )
   S
ROSLAVETZ, N. A. (1881-   )
   Ens
ROSSINI, G. (1792-1868)   VV   D
   trans Bochsa, Labarre, Magistretti, Parish-Alvars, Steil,
   Suerth, Thomas
ROTA, N. (1911-   )
   Ens (1937)
ROTHSCHILD, W. DE (19th century French composer)
   trans Carusi
ROUSSEAU, S. A. (1853-1904)
   "Fantaisie" for chromatic harp and string quartet.
ROUSSEL, A. (1869-1937)
   "Serenade" for violin, flute, viola, cello and harp, Op. 30.
RUBINSTEIN, A. (1830-1894)   A   D
   trans Hasselmans, Pinto, Salzedo, Snoer
   Reco—"Romance"—Sassoli, S—V 4570.
RUNDNAGEL, K. (1835-1911)
   S
RUTA, R. (1876-1919)
   S; Ens—duets; trans
SAAL, M. (1882-   )
   S

SELECTED COMPOSERS, COMPOSITIONS AND RECORDINGS

SAINT QUENTIN, G. DE (contemporary French composer)
Ens—two and four harps

SAINT-SAENS, C. (1835-1921)   VV   VI   B1   D
IIIx
S; trans Choisnel, Hasselmans, N. S. Miller, Pinto, Roques,
Snoer, Verdalle; Ens—"Concertpiece" for harp and or-
chestra, Op. 154 (1918) ; "Fantasie" for violin and harp,
Op. 124 (1907).
Reco—"Fantasie for harp" Op. 95—Laskine, S—G DA5010.
—"The Swan"—Lorenzi, harp; Torch, organ—C 418M.

SALVI, ALBERTO   VIII*   IX   *   B2
S; trans; Classical trans for Ens; Reco for V (see Bishop,
Chopin, Flotow, Foster, Nevin, Parish-Alvars)

SALZEDO, CARLOS (1885-   )   VIII*   IX   #   Ix
IIx   A   B1   B2   B3   C   D   VIx
Numerous S; trans; Classical trans; M (with Lawrence) ;
E; Stu; "Art of Modulation" (with Lawrence) ; Ens—
numerous works for from two to seven harps, and for harp
and other instruments, including: "Enchanted Isle" for
harp and orchestra; "Four Preludes to the Afternoon of
a Telephone" for two harps (1921) ; "Preamble et Jeux"
for harp, four winds, five strings (1929) ; Reco—solo
and Ens for V, CM (see Debussy, Rameau, Trio de Luce)
Reco—"Chanson Dans la Nuit"—CM 283 (album) ; Rear-
don, S—Sch 5507; Lawrence, S—C 68284.
—"Concerto for Harp and Woodwinds"—Ens—CM
283.
—"Memories of a Clock", "Pirouetting Music Box",
"Behind the Barracks", "Rocking Horse", "On
Donkey Back", "Rain Drops"—S—V 14871.
—"Scintillation"—S—V
—"Whirlwind"—S—C DB565.

SAMAZEUILH, G. (1877-   )
S

SAMINSKY, L. (1882-   )
"Chassidic Suite" for violin, cello solo, piano or harp (1937).

SAMMARTINI, G. (1700-1775)   C
trans Grandjany

SASSOLI, ADA (1887-1946)   VIII*   *
trans; many early S Reco for V (see Bach, Debussy, Hasselmans, Mozart, Rubinstein, Zabel)

SAUVAGE, A.   D
S

THE HARP

SCARLATTI, A. (1659-1725)
  trans Magistretti, Pinto, Renie
SCHAEFFER, A.
  S; Stu; trans; M; Ens—"Harp prelude" on Mozart's "Ave
  Verum Corpus" (1891)
SCHAPOSHNIKOV, A. (1888-   )
  "Sonata" for flute and harp (1924).
SCHMIDT, E.
  E revised by Jamet (1937)
SCHMITT, F. (1870-   )
  S for chromatic harp; Ens—"Suite en Rocaille" for flute,
  violin, viola and harp, Op. 68, (1935).
SCHOENBERG, A. (1874-   )
  "Herzgewächse" for voice, celeste, harmonium and harp,
  Op. 20.
SCHUBERT, F. (1797-1828)   IIIx   A
  trans Alberti, Beon, Dilling, Fels, Macquarrie, Renie, Snoer,
  Zamara
  Reco—"Moment Musical"—Renie, S—D 20518.
    —"Ave Maria"—soprano with harp accompaniment—
    V 55052; Primrose, viola and S. Goossens, harp—
    C 7278M.
SCHUECKER, E. (1860-1911)   *   VIII   IIx
  Numerous S; Stu; E; Ens; Orchestral Stu; A (Naderman);
  trans
  Reco—"Concert Mazurka"—Warner, S—V
SCHUETZE, CHARLES   A
  S; Early S (see Dubez) and Ens Reco for C—Ens with violin,
  cello; with flute and cello; with violin and flute.
SCHUMANN, R. (1810-1856)   A   B1   C   D
  trans Alberti, Beon, Coeur, Hasselmans, Hunter, M. Miller,
  Renie, Robinson, Ruta, Samm, Snoer; Ens
  Reco—"Songs by Robert Schumann"—Thebom, mezzo-so-
    prano; Hughes, piano; Newell, harp—V MO 1187.
SCHYTTE, L. (1850-1909)
  Ens
SCOTT, P. (1790-1856)
  S; trans
SERRAO, P. (1830-after 1870)
  Ens
SIBELIUS, J. (1865-   )   VV   VI
  Reco—"Pastorale"—Dilling, S—C 17107.

SELECTED COMPOSERS, COMPOSITIONS AND RECORDINGS

SINDING, C. (1856-1941)
trans David
SISTER F. THERESE   B2   C
S
SISTER M. ATTRACTA COFFEY
Ir M (1903)
SISTER M. CHARLES   IIx
A; trans
SMYTHE, DAME E. (1858-   )
"Four de Regnier Songs" for voice, harp and other instruments accompanying.
SNOER, J. (1868-   )   VIII   B1   B2   B3   D
Numerous S; Ens; Orchestral Stu; M; A; Ir S
SODERO, D.   B1   B2   D
S; Ir S; Ens
SOULAGE, M. (1894-   )
"Legende" for flute, oboe and harp.
SOWERBY, L. (1895-   )
"Concerto" for harp and orchestra.
SPELMAN, T. M. (1891-   )   VIx
Ens—"Poeme" after Gautier's 'Pavillion sur L'Eau' for flute, violin, viola, cello and harp; "Rondo" for flute and harp.
SPOHR, L. (1784-1859)   V
S; Numerous Ens
STAHL, W. (1896-   )
S; Ens—"Piece" for harp and strings (1936).
STANDING, V.   B3   D
S
STCHERBATCHEFF, V. (1889-   )
"Nonet" for string quartet, harp, piano, violin solo, dance and light.
STEIBELT, D. (1765-1823)
"Grand Concerto in E♭ major" for harp and orchestra.
STEPHEN, R. (1887-1915)
"Musick" for string quintet, piano and harp.
STOCKHAUSEN, F. (1792-1868)
S
STOKOWSKI, L. (1887-   )
"Dithyrambe" for flute, cello and harp (1917).
STRAUSS, J. (1825-1899)
trans Macquarrie

[149]

THE HARP

STUNTZ, J. H. (1793-1859)
Ens—duets
SUERTH, PAUL   D
trans; Early Ens Reco for C—Ens with violin and flute.
SUESSE, D.
"Young Man with a Harp" for harp and orchestra
Reco—Reardon, harp; Suesse, piano; Morehouse, drums—
Sch set 8.
TAYLOR, G.   IIx
trans of airs
TEDESCHI, L. M. (1867-after 1908)   D
S; Stu; E; Ens—"Suite" for violin, cello and harp.
Reco—Two pieces—Gandolfi, S—C CXQ16492.
THOMAS, J. (1826-1913)   *   A   D   IIIx   VIx
Numerous S; Numerous trans Welsh airs; Stu; Ens—con-
certos in E♭, B♭, for harp and orchestra, duets.
Reco—"Autumn"—Lapitino, S—V 20426.
THOMAS, V.
Ens—Two pieces for strings and harp (1937)
THOME, F. (1850-1909)
trans Hasselmans, Martenot; Ens—"Legende" for harp and
orchestra, Op. 122.
TORGERSON, H. S.   C   D
S; trans
TOURNIER, M. (1879-   )   *   A   IIIx   VIx
Numerous S; A (1926); Numerous Ens—"Feerie—prelude
and dance" for harp and strings (1921).
Reco—"Grey Donkeys on Road to El-Azib"—Dilling, S—C
—"Vers la Source dans la Bois"—Zighera, S—C 2097.
TRAMONTI, E. (1879-now deceased)   VIII*
trans
TRIO DE LUCE—flute, cello and harp.
Reco for C (see Beethoven, Mendelssohn, Widor).
TRNECEK, H. (1858-1914)
S; trans; Ens—duets
TSCHAIKOWSKY, P. I. (1840-1893)   VV   VI   IIIx
trans Maganini, Pinto, Salzedo
TYRE, M.   C
A (Bach—1942)
VAN VACTOR, D. (1906-   )
"Concerto Grosso" for three flutes, harp and orchestra
(1935).

SELECTED COMPOSERS, COMPOSITIONS AND RECORDINGS

VENETIAN TRIO—violin, cello and harp
  Early Ens Reco for V.
VERDALLE, G.   A   B1   B3   D
  S; Ens
VERDI, G. (1813-1901)   I   VV   D
  trans Balfi, Bellotta, Bovio, Chatterton, Cheshire, Oberthur,
  Puzone, Stanek, Taylor, Thomas, Zamara.
VERNIER, J. A. (1769-1795)
  S; Ens—quartet, trio
VIERNE, L. (1870-1937)
  S
VINEE, A. (-1912)
  "Trio Serenade" for flute, cor anglaise (or oboe) and harp.
VITO, EDWARD   VIII*
  trans; Reco—Popular music for D, V
  Reco—"Dick Leibert at the Organ"—V P164 (see MILLS).
    —"Moon Love—Collection of Tschaikowsky Themes"
      —harp with rhythm accompaniment—D A301.
VITO, JOSEPH   VIII   B2   C   D
  S; trans; Stu (1946) ; Reco with symphony orchestra for V.
VIVALDI, A. (1676-1741)
  trans Gillman
VOLKMAN, R. (1815-1883)
  "Schlummerlied" for harp, clarinet and horn, Op. 76.
VON HOLST, G. (1874-1934)
  S; Ens.
WACHTMEISTER, A. R. (1865-   )
  S
WAEFELGHEM, L. VON (1840-1908)
  "Soir d'Automne" for viola d'amour and harp.
WAGENAAR, B. (1894-   )
  Ens—"Three Songs from the Chinese" for voice, flute, harp
    and piano (1921) ; "Triple Concerto" for flute, harp,
    cello and orchestra (1935).
WAGNER, J. (1900-   )
  "Concertino" for harp and orchestra (premiere Feb. 1949)
WAGNER, R. (1813-1883)   VV   VI
  trans Dilling, Fels, Kastner, Oberthur, Roques, Salzedo,
  Schuecker.

[151]

WARNER, GENEVIEVE
Early S Reco (see Schuecker)

WEBER, C. M. VON (1786-1826)
trans Bochsa, Snoer, Zeller

WEBERN, A. VON (1883-1945)
"Five Sacred Songs" for soprano, flute, clarinet, trumpet, harp and double bass, Op. 15.

WESTERHOUT, N. (1862-1898)
S

WHITE, P. (1895-   )
Reco—"Sea Chanty"—Phillips, harp; Hilsberg and Rudens, violins; Mayes, cello; Roens, viola; Torelli, bass
—CM MX259.

WIDOR, C. M. (1845-1931)   VIx
"Chorale and Variations" for harp and orchestra, Op. 74 (1899).
Reco—"Serenade"—Trio de Luce

WIEGAND, A.   IIIx
Ens

WIGHTMAN, F.   IX
trans

WILM, N. VON (1834-1911)
Ens—"Concertpiece" for harp and orchestra, Op. 122 (1892) ; Duo for harp and violin, Op. 156.

WOHLFAHRT, H. (1797-1883)   IIx
M; Stu; E

WOOD, H. (1869-   )   D
trans Macquarrie

WRIGHT, T. H.   *   VII
S; Stu

WURMSER-DELCOURT, L.   VII
S; M

ZABEL, A. H. (1835-1910)   *   B1   D   VIx
S; M; Ens—"Concerto in C Minor" for harp and orchestra, Op. 35 (1902).
Reco—"Chanson de Pecheur"—Sassoli, S—
—"La Source"—Renie, S—D-O 25050; Sassoli, S—V 70031.

ZAMARA, A. (1829-1901)   *   VIII
Numerous S; M; Ens

SELECTED COMPOSERS, COMPOSITIONS AND RECORDINGS

ZANDONAI, R. (1883-   )
> Ens—"Sonata Medievale" for strings, two horns, harp and cello solo; "Ave Maria" for women's voices, harp and strings.

ZIGHERA, BERNARD (1904-   )   VIII*   #
> S Reco for C (see Tournier)

ZIMMER, NELLIE   VIII*
> Early Ens Reco for V

ZINGEL, R. E. (1876-   )   B1
> S

ZIPOLI, D. (1675-1726)
> trans Gillman, Magistretti, Pinto, Renie.

CHAPTER V

Selected Harp Solos for School Assemblies, Plays and Programs

THIS SECTION has been compiled with the aim of facilitating the use of the harp in school assemblies and other school activities. For convenient reference, the harp solos presented here are grouped under four general headings:

   A. Solos for special school programs—arranged seasonally by the months of the school year (not in monthly order of progressive study).

   B. Solo harp music for theatrical productions—arranged in three categories:
      1. Fantasy Music
      2. Incidental Music
      3. Dance Music

   C. Study pieces for the harp—grouped in order of grades of difficulty.

   D. Program music solos—including favorite airs and familiar ballads. As in the above section, the pieces are grouped in order of grade of difficulty.

The solo music included here is graded in the following manner:

   (II) Easy pieces. The Roman numeral (I) following the Roman numeral (II) grade, indicates that this piece could also be used as a *first* piece for the very young harpist.

   (II-III) More advanced easy pieces—requiring more use of pedals and more difficult finger placement than pieces of grade (II).

   (III) Medium pieces—requiring moderate use of pedals; arpeggios, glissandos, and harmonics.

   (IV) More difficult pieces—requiring greater technical skill and musical understanding; more extensive coordination of pedals; and more difficult arpeggios, tempo changes, etc., and special effects.

[155]

This list does not comprise the complete repertoire for the student harpist; it is only representative of the music available. Whenever possible, the date of publication of the composition, as well as the name of the publisher and number of pages, has been included. This information appears directly under the title of the composition and the name of the composer.

In sections "A" and "B", the grades of the solos are indicated by the Roman numeral appearing to the right of each title. In sections "C" and "D", the Roman numeral at the head of each group of solos indicates the grade.

Names of publishers are abbreviated as follows:

  And—Andre, Germany
  AAM—American Academy of Music, New York
  AMP—Associated Music Publishers, N. Y. C.
  Ash—Ashdown, England
  Bel—Belwin, N. Y. C.
  Bes—Bessel, Germany, Russia
  Bl—Black, Los Angeles, California
  Bla—Blanchi, Italy
  B & H—Breitkopf & Hartel, Germany
  Cam—Cameron, Washington, D. C.
  Car—Carisch, S. A., Italy
  C F—Carl Fischer, N. Y. C.
  Chal—Chalmers, Akron, Ohio
  Chap—Chappell, N. Y. C.
  Ches—Chester, England
  Cla—Clark, Syracuse, New York
  Cos—Costallat, France
  Cra—Cramer, England
  Cz—Cranz, Germany
  Dei—Deiss, France
  Dem—Demets, E., France
  Dit—Ditson, Boston, N. Y. C.
  Dur—Durand, France
  E A—Emil Ascher, N. Y. C.
  E M—Edition Musicus, N. Y. C.
  EMl'U—Editions de Musique de l'Urss, Russia
  E-V—Elkan-Vogel, Philadelphia, Pennsylvania
  F D—F. Durdilly, France
  Gie—Giessel, Germany

SELECTED HARP SOLOS FOR SCHOOL ASSEMBLIES

G & B—Gould & Bolttler, England
G & T—Gay & Tenton, France
Ham—Hamelle, France
Heu—Heugel & Cie, France
Hof—Hofmeister, Germany
H & R—Hutchings & Romer, England
Int—International, N. Y. C.
JJ—Jean Joubert, France
Le—Leede, Germany
Led—Leduc, France
Lem—Lemoine, France
Leu—Leuckart, Germany
Mers—Mersburger, Germany
Mk—Marks, N. Y. C.
Mur—Murdoch, Murdoch & Co., Scotland
Od—Odell, Boston, Mass.
PML—Parnasse Musical Locute, Que., Canada
Pres—Presser, Philadelphia, Pa.
R. B. & W.—Riker, Brown & Wellington, Boston, Mass.
RJ—R. Jzzo, Italy
Rou—Rouhier, France
Roz—Rozsavolgyi, Hungary
S-C—Sprague-Coleman, N. Y. C.
Sch—Schirmer, N. Y. C.
Scho—Schott, Germany
Sen—Senart, France
Sim—Simon, Germany
SN—Schmid, Nachfolger, Germany
SSM—Schott's Söhne, Germany
UE—Universal Edition, Austria
Wil—Wilshire, Los Angeles, Cal.
W-S—White-Smith, N. Y. C.
Zim—Zimmerman, Germany

A. Solos for special school programs—arranged seasonally by
the months of the school year (not in monthly order of
progressive study). Solos are listed alphabetically by the
titles.

SEPTEMBER—Music for autumn
   "Automne"—Grandjany   (IV)
      E-V   1927   4 p
   "Autumn"—J. Thomas   (IV)
      H & R   1912   11 p

THE HARP

"Feuilles d'Automne"—Renie   (III)
     Rou   1912   4 p
OCTOBER—International Program
AMERICA
     "Largo" from "New World" Symphony—Dvorak   (III)
         from "Original Compositions and Adaptations for Harp"
         album edited by Gertrude Ina Robinson.
         CF   3 p
ARABIA
     "Dance Arabe"—DeStefano   (III)
         from "Petite Suite Orientale"
         Int   1914   2 p
CHINA
     "Old Chinese Song"—Grandjany   (IV)
         Mk   4 p
EGYPT
     "L'Egyptienne"—Rameau-Renie   (III)
         Dur   4 p
ENGLAND
     "Drink To Me Only With Thine Eyes"   (III)
         from "Excerpts and Solos for Small Harp"
         album edited by Gertrude Ina Robinson
         CF   1913   3 p
FRANCE
     "Et Ron Ron Ron Petit Patapon"—Grandjany   (III)
         E-V   1941   4 p
     "Vieille Chanson Normande"—Godefroid   (II-III)
         from "Musical Thoughts" album—Volume I
         FD   2 p
INDIA
     "Serenade Hindoue"—DiStefano   (II-III)
         from "Petite Suite Orientale"
         Int   1914   2 p
ITALY
     "Santa Lucia"—N. S. Miller   (III)
         Bel   2 p
     "Souvenir d'Italie"—DiStefano   (II-III)
         Int   1914   4 p
RUSSIA
     "Cossack Dance"—Brittain   (III)
         from "Asiatic Sketches"
         Int   1922   2½ p

SELECTED HARP SOLOS FOR SCHOOL ASSEMBLIES

"Song of the Volga Boatman"—Hass   (III)
    Int   1922   6 p
WALES
    "The Ash Grove"—Black   (II-III)
        Bl   1942   3 p
NOVEMBER—Music for Thanksgiving
    "Angelus"—Renie   (II-III)
        from "Album Leaves" by Renie revised by Grandjany
        Mk   1943   2 p
    "Divine Calme"—Godefroid   (II-III)
        from "Musical Thoughts" album—vol. I
        FD   2 p
    "Prayer"—Poenitz   (II) (I)
        Sim   1902   2 p
DECEMBER—Christmas Music
    "Adeste Fideles—Concert Variations"—Salzedo   (IV)
        E-V   1938   5 p
    "An Old Christmas Song—Silent Night"—Grandjany (III)
        E-V   1930   4 p
    "Ave Maria"—Schubert-Macquarrie   (III)
        Bel   1942   5 p
    "Berceuse de Noel"—Paret   (II) (I)
        S-C   1939   1 p
    "Holy Night" (Silent Night, Holy Night)   (II-III)
        from "Excerpts and Solos for Small Harp"
        album edited by Robinson
        CF   1913   2 p
    "Jingle Bells"—Salzedo   (III)
        E-V   1945   2 p
    "Noel Provincial"—Grandjany   (II-III)
        Mk   1941   5 p
    "Silent Night—Concert Variations"—Salzedo   (III)
        E-V   1938   2 p
    "Silent Night, Holy Night"—Grandjany   (IV)
        E-V   1930   4 p
    "Six Noels"—Tournier   (III)
        Lem   1929   Album—8 p
CHRISTMAS TOY MUSIC
    "Berceuse de Dolly"—Faure   (III)
        from "Album of Solo Pieces" edited by David—Vol. I
        Sch   1916   4 p
    "March of the Marionettes"—Rogers   (II) (I)
        CF   2 p

"Music Box"—Poenitz (III)
from "Album of Solo Pieces" edited by David—Vol. I
    Sch   1916   2 p
"Pirouetting Music Box"—Salzedo (II-III)
from "Short Stories in Music" album—series II
    E-V   1935   2 p
JANUARY—Winter Weather Music
"Drifting Snow"—Cameron (II) (I)
    Cam   1939   2 p
"Winter"—Hoberg (III)
Suite from "Log Cabin Sketches"
    Dit   1920   14 p
FEBRUARY—Famous Composers Birthday Program
Handel—born Feb. 23, 1685
    "Harmonious Blacksmith" (IV)
    transcribed for harp solo by Salzedo
    E-V   1936   6 p
Mendelssohn—born Feb. 3, 1809
    "On Wings of Song" (II-III)
    transcribed for harp solo by N. S. Miller
    Bel   3 p
Chopin—born Feb. 22, 1810
    "Preludes—No. 6 in B minor, No. 11 in
    B major" (III)
    transcribed for harp solo by Renie
    G & T   1928   2 p
MARCH—St. Patrick's Day Music (March 17)
"Believe Me If All Those Endearing Young Charms"—
    transcribed by: Cheshire (III)
    Cra   5 p
        Salzedo (II-III)
    CF   1925   3 p
"Irish Gems"—F. B. Chatterton (II-III)
    Alla Preludio, Moll Roone, Noran Kista, Domhnall
    Ash   4 p
"Last Rose of Summer"—
    transcribed by: Cheshire (III)
    Cra   5 p
        Salzedo (II-III)
    CF   3 p
        Schueltze (II-III)
    Int   1914   5 p

SELECTED HARP SOLOS FOR SCHOOL ASSEMBLIES

"Medley of Irish Melodies"—Moore   (II-III)
    arranged by Robinson, from "Excerpts and Solos for Small
    Harp" album edited by Robinson
    CF   1913   4 p

APRIL—Music for Spring

"Melodie in F"—A. Rubinstein
    transcribed by: Hasselmans   (III)
    Ham   4 p
                    Salzedo   (III)
    CF   1925   4 p
"Spring Song"—Mendelssohn-Cheshire   (III)
    Dit   1912   4 p
"Spring Time"—Albeniz-Renie   (IV)
    Led   1922   3 p
"Spring Time"—Rogers   (II)
    Dit   1922   2 p

MUSIC FOR EASTER

"Priere"—Godefroid   (II)
    from "Musical Thoughts" album Vol. I.
    FD   2 p
"Prayer"—Hasselmans   (IV)
    from "Album of Solo Pieces" edited by David—Vol. I
"Consecration"—Robinson   (II)
    from "Original Compositions and Adaptations for Harp"
    album edited by Robinson.
    CF   3 p
"Priere"—Verdalle ·   (III)
    FD   1898   3 p

MAY—Music for May Day

"Daisy"—Pinto   (III)
    Int   1915   10 p
"Lily"—Pinto   (II)
    Int   1919   3 p

MEMORIAL DAY MUSIC

"Hymne a la Paix"—Godefroid   (II-III)
    from "Musical Thoughts" album Vol. I
    FD   2 p
"Behind the Barracks"—Salzedo   (III)
    from "Short Stories in Music" album series II
    E-V   1935   2 p

JUNE—Music for Summer

"Clear Sky"—Achard-Prothin   (IV)
   Int   5 p
"By the Brook"—Boisdoffre-J. Vito   (III)
   Bel   1942   6 p
"Summer"—Hoberg   (III)
   Suite from "Log Cabin Sketches"
   Dit   1920   13 p
"Idyll"—Loukine   (II)
   Int   1913   2 p
"Skipping Rope"—Salzedo   (III)
   from "Short Stories in Music"album series II
   E-V   1935   3 p
"In the Garden"—Schuetze   (III)
   Sch   1911   5 p
"Happy Farmer"—Schumann   (II)
   from "Excerpts and Solos for Small Harp"
   album edited by Robinson
   CF   1913   2 p
"Rising of the Lark"—Thomas   (III)
   Ash   8 p
"Summer"—J. Thomas   (III)
   G & B   9 p

B. Solo harp music for theatrical productions

The music of the harp is particularly well suited to the needs of school theatrical productions. The harp may be included in the orchestral ensemble used to provide entre' acte music, and it may be used to even better advantage in providing accompaniments for vocal or dance numbers, or for special atmospheric effects. For purposes of the latter group, the harp (used alone, or with a small number of strings or woodwinds) may be placed back-stage. Back-stage use of the harp is most effective from an audience stand-point, and it also simplifies the matter of cueing in the music.

For reference purposes the harp solos in this section are arranged in three catagories:

   1. FANTASY MUSIC—including: Dreams, Romances and Reveries; Fairy and Elf Music; Mysterious Music; Water Music; Miscellany.

2. INCIDENTAL MUSIC—including: Barcarolle; Impromptu; Intermezzo; Lullaby; Nocturne; Prelude; Serenade; Miscellany.

3. DANCE MUSIC—including: Early Dances; Minuet; Waltz; Miscellany.

Any discussion of the theatrical possibilities of the harp would hardly be complete without mention of the dramatic effectiveness of the *glissando*. For the quick entrance or exit of spirits or sprites; for mysterious shimmering effects; and for the impression of the intangible, the glissando is supreme. Generally speaking, the glissandos of the major chords are bright and guileless. The dominant seventh chord and whole tone scale glissandos give a "prelude" effect, while the glissando of the pentatonic scale sounds very final. The glissandos of the diminished seventh and the augmented chords sound mysterious (the latter more so than the former).

The glissando must be used with discretion! In the tasteful use of this effect lies its charm.

* * *

As in division "A" of this section, the name of the publisher and the number of pages of the composition, and (whenever possible) the date of publication, are included under the title of the composition and the name of the composer. The grade of each solo is indicated by the Roman numeral in parentheses to the right of the name of the composer. Solos are arranged alphabetically by titles.

1. FANTASY MUSIC
   Dreams, Romances and Reveries—
      "Dreaming"—Posse   (III)
         from "Six Little Pieces" album
         Zim   1910   2 p
     "En Reve"—Verdalle   (III)
         Led   1905   4 p
     "Reverie"—Hasselmans   (II-III)
         from "Three Little Pieces" album
         Dur   2 p

"Reverie"—Holy (III)
   Int   1917   4 p
"Romance"—Snoer (II-III)
   Zim   1913   4 p
"Romance sans Paroles"—Faure-Hasselmans (III)
   Ham   2 p
"Un Moment Heureux"—Zabel (III)
   Bes   3 p
   (Also included in "Album of Solo Pieces" compiled by David.)
"Vision"—Verdalle (II-III)
   Int   1913   3 p
"Vision in B*b*"—Chalmers (II-III)
   Chal   3 p
Fairy and Elf Music—
"Kewpie's Drill"—Rogers (II)
   CF   1917   1 p
"Fairies' Dream"—Robinson (II-III)
   from "Excerpts and Solos for Small Harp"
   album by Robinson
   CF   1913   3 p
Mysterious Music—
"March of the Gnomes"—Robinson (II)
   CF   1913   2 p
"Chanson dans la nuit"—Salzedo (III)
   from "Method for the Harp" Salzedo-Lawrence
   Sch   1929   5 p
"The Chrysanthemum"—Britain (III)
   from "Asiatic Sketches"
   Int   1922   2 p
"L'Oiseau Prophete"—Schumann-Renie (IV)
   G & T   1928   3 p
"Suspense Cues"—Mills (III)
   from "Harp Cues for Radio" album by Verlye Mills
   EA   1943   many ½ page cues
"Will-o'-the Wisp"—Hasselmans (IV)
   Dur   7 p
Water Music—
"At the Brook"—Loukine (II)
   Int   1914   2 p
"La Cascade"—Oberthur (III)
   Ash   8 p

SELECTED HARP SOLOS FOR SCHOOL ASSEMBLIES

"Murmuring Waves"—Robinson   (II-III)
    from "Original Compositions and Adaptations"
    album edited by Robinson
    CF   3 p

Miscellany—
"Ballade"—Hasselmans   (IV)
    Led   10 p
"Ecstasy"—Cheshire   (III)
    Dit   1912   4 p
"Elegy in G"—Zingel   (IV)
    Mers   1929   10 p
"Fantasie"—Saint-Saens   (IV)
    Dur   15 p
"Fraîcheur"—Salzedo   (III)
    Sch   1933   3 p
"La Harpe Eolienne"—Godefroid   (IV)
    Dei   5 p
"Impressione"—Sodero   (III)
    Int   1917   5 p
"Improvisations"—Snoer   (IV)
    Scho   22 p
"Rondo Capriccioso"—Cella   (IV)
    Int   1919   10 p
"Rouet"—Hasselmans   (II-III)
    from "Three Little Pieces" album
    Dur   3 p
"Song of the Winds"—Chalmers   (II-III)
    Chal   1929   3 p
"Twilight Murmurs"—Cheshire   (II-III)
    Dit   1912   4 p

2. INCIDENTAL MUSIC
Barcarolle—
"Barcarolle"—Grandjany   (II)
    from "Three Easy Pieces" album
    Mk   1943   2p
"Barcarolle"—Hasselmans   (III)
    Dur   7 p
"Barcarolle"—Roger-Ducasse   (IV)
    Dur   1907   8 p
Impromptu—
"Melodie Impromptu"—Sister F. Therese   (III)
    CF   1937   7 p

"Impromptu"—Loukine   (IV)
    Int   1914   5 p
"Josephine"—Navone   (III)
    Bla   3 p
"Impromptu"—J. Vito   (IV)
    Bel   1942   9 p
Intermezzo—
"Intermezzo Romantic"—Kastner   (III)
    Int   1913   5 p
"Intermezzo"—Loukine   (II-III)
    Int   1914   4 p
"Capriccio Marcial und Intermezzo"—Snoer   (II-III)
    Zim   1913   3 p
Lullaby—
"Berceuse"—Sodero   (II-III)
    Int   1912   3 p
"Lullaby"—Brahms-Salzedo   (II-III)
    E-V   1935   2 p
"Lullaby"—Kastner   (II-III)
    Int   1913   5 p
"Petite Berceuse"—Pinto   (II)
    Int   1914   3 p
Nocturne
"Nocturne"—Beon   (IV)
    Cos   1907   4 p
"Nocturne"—Grandjany   (II)
    from "Three Easy Pieces" album
    Mk   1943   2p
Prelude—
"Introspection"—Salzedo   (IV)
    CF   1924   9 p
"Preludes"—Grandjany   (II-III)
    Allegretto, Moderato, Allegretto
    Sen   1921   5 p
Serenade—
"Scherzino"—Salvi   (III)
    Int   1922   3 p
"Serenade"—Robinson   (II-III)
    from "Original Compositions and Adaptations"
    album edited by Robinson
    CF   5 p

"Serenade"—Salvi   (III)
    Int   1923   3 p
"Serenade Capricciosa"—Pinto   (III)
    Int   1913   4 p

Miscellany—
"Grand Arpeggio"—Chalmers   (II-III)
    Chal   3 p
"In the Twilight Hour"—Oberthur   (II-III)
    Ash   4 p
"Le Matin"—DiStefano   (III)
    Int   1917   3 p

3. DANCE MUSIC

Early Dances—
"Danses d'Autrefois"—Renie   (II-III)
    from "Album Leaves" by Renie revised by Grandjany
    Mk   1943   2 p
"Gavotte" from "Armide"—Gluck-Salzedo   (III)
    Sch   1937   3 p
"Gavotte"—Posse   (II-III)
    from "Six Little Pieces" album
    Zim   1910   4 p

Minuet—
"Menuet"—Hasselmans   (III)
    Dur   5 p
"Minuetto" from "Don Giovanni"—Mozart-N. S. Miller
                                                       (II-III)
    Bel   3 p
"Minuet"—Beethoven   (III)
    from "Album of Solo Pieces" edited by David—Vol. I
    Sch   1916   2 p
"Minuet"—Robinson   (II)
    from "Original Compositions and Adaptations"
    edited by Robinson
    CF   2 p

Waltz—
"Butterfly Waltz"—Robinson   (II-III)
    from "Excerpts and Solos for Small Harp"
    album edited by Robinson
    CF   1913   2 p

[167]

"Grazioso"—Chalmers (II-III)
    Chal   1928   3 p
"La Rosa Waltz"—Dussek (II)
    Ash   2 p
"Valse Romantique"—Debussy-Coeur (IV)
    JJ   1929   6 p
"Valse Caprice"—Snoer (II)
    Leu   1908   4 p
"Valse Caprice"—Verdalle (III)
    Zim   1903   6 p
"Valse Isabel"—Rogers (II)
    CF   1917   2 p

Miscellany—

"Caprice"—Nicoletta (III)
    Int   1918   3 p
"Dancing Shadows"—Standing (II-III)
    Int   1914   4 p
"Danza Fantastica"—Cella (III)
    Int   1919   3 p
"Gipsy Fire Dance"—Chalmers (II-III)
    Chal   1928   3 p
"Mazurka"—Posse (IV)
    Zim   1905   5 p

C. Study pieces for the harp—grouped in order of grades of difficulty. Solos are arranged alphabetically by composers.

Grade II

"Bagatelles"—Grandjany
    Mk   1941   4 p
        Chanson
        Cloches (Bells)
        Melancolie
"Minuet in Eb"—Mozart-Pinto
    Int   1916   3 p
"Song Without Words"—Posse
    Zim   1910   1 p
"Petite Etude"—Schumann-M. Miller
    CF   1925   3 p
See also Section III, Chapter II—Albums for the Beginning Student—Very Young.

Grade II-III

"First Prelude"—Chalmers
    Chal   1924   3 p

SELECTED HARP SOLOS FOR SCHOOL ASSEMBLIES

"Largo"—Handel-Bedell
  PML   1946   2 p
"Prelude in Bb Minor"—Loukine
  Int   1914   2 p
"Gavotte"—Rameau-Salzedo
  Sch   1923   9 p
See also Section III, Chapter II—Albums for the Beginning Student—Intermediate.

Grade III

"Prelude in Db Major"—J. S. Bach-Tyre
  from "Bach for the Harp" album transcribed by Marjorie Tyre
  E-V   1942   3 p
"Solfeggietto"—K.P.E. Bach-N. S. Miller
  Bel   3 p
"Andante" from "Sonata Passionata"—Beethoven-Robinson from "Original Compositions and Adaptations for the Harp" album edited by Robinson.
  CF   5 p
"Giga"—A. Corelli-Salzedo
  Sch   1923   3 p
"Tema con variazione"—A. Corelli-Pinto
  Od   1926   3 p
Harp Solo (Cadenza) from "Lucia di Lammermoor"—Donizetti-Salzedo.
  E-V   1934   3 p
"Chaconne"—Durand-Salzedo
  Sch   1923   9 p
"Au Monastère"—Hasselmans
  Dur   4 p
"Scherzo"—Leonardo
  E-V   1935   5 p
"Rigaudon"—Rameau-Salzedo
  Sch   1942   4 p
"Cortège"—Salzedo   2 p
"La Desirade"—Salzedo   3 p
  from "Method for the Harp"—Lawrence-Salzedo
  Sch   1929
"Prelude in D Minor"—Sister F. Therese
  CF   1937   5 p

"Bourree"—Torgerson
    Dur   1927   3 p
"Twenty Etudes"—J. Vito
    first ten
    Bel   1946   40 p
Grade IV
"Bourree" from Partita I—J. S. Bach-Salzedo
    Sch   1923   3 p
"La Melodieuse"—Daquin-Renie
    G & T   1928   2 p
"La Victoire"—Duphly-Renie
    G & T   1928   3 p
"La Fille aux Cheveux de Lin"—Debussy-Grandjany
    Dur   1910   2 p
"Sonata in C Minor"—Pescetti-Salzedo
    Sch   1937   10 p
"Contentment"—Torgerson
    Dur   1927   6 p
"Twenty Etudes"—J. Vito
    11 to 20
    Bel   1946   40 p

D. Program music solos—including favorite airs and familiar ballads. As in the previous section, the pieces are grouped in order of grade of difficulty. Solos are arranged alphabetically by composers.

Grade II
"Ballade"—Cameron   (I)
    Cam   1938   3 p
"March Majestic"—Chalmers
    Chal   1924   3 p
"Londonderry Air"—Paret   (I)
    S-C   1939   1 p
"Moonlight"—Paret   (I)
    S-C   1939   1 p
"Melody"—Parkhurst
    from "Excerpts and Solos for Small Harp"
    album edited by Robinson
    CF   1913   2 p
"Vivace"—Parkhurst
    from "Original Compositions and Adaptations"
    album edited by Robinson
    CF   2 p

SELECTED HARP SOLOS FOR SCHOOL ASSEMBLIES

"Song Without Words"—Posse
    Le   2 p
"Waltz Albania"—Rogers
    Cla   1910   4 p

Grade II-III

"Valse in A♭"—Brahms-N. S. Miller
    Bel   2 p
"From the Land of the Sky Blue Water"—Cadman-Z. Clark
    W-S   1937   4 p
"Glamour Suite—Under the Rainbow"—Chalmers
    Magic Fountain
    A Procession of the Magi
    Dance Under the Rainbow
    Chal   1939   5 p
"Remembrance"—Cheshire
    Dit   1930   4 p
"Two Songs Without Words"—Dubez
    Cz   5 p
"Famous Melodies" album of five Stephen Foster melodies arranged by Riley
    Wil   1940   13 p
"Amaryllis"—Ghys-N. S. Miller
    Bel   5 p
"Consolation"—Mendelssohn-Hunter
    Bel   2 p
"Chanson de Guillot-Martin"—Perilhou-M. Miller
    CF   1925   4 p
"Estrellita"—Ponce-Black
    Bl   1942   6 p
"Esquisse"—Renie-Grandjany
    from "Album Leaves"
    Mk   1943   2 p
"The Tear"—A. Rubinstein-Hasselmans
    Ham   2 p
"Evening Hour"—Standing
    Int   1912   4 p
"Butterflies"—Verdalle
    Int   1913   3 p

Grade III

"Annie Laurie"—Cheshire
    Dit   1912   3 p

THE HARP

"Chanson d'Orient"—Dubois-Renie
   Led   4 p
"Humoresque"—Dvorak-Pinto
   Int   1919   3 p
"From a Railway Carriage"—Forst
   EM   1944   3 p
"Windy Nights"—Forst
   EM   1942   5 p
"Promenade"—I. Freed
   Bel   1942   4 p
"Schöne Erinnerung"—Hahn
   And   5 p
"Largo"—Handel-Hunter
   Bel   3 p
"Gondoliers"—Hasselmans
   Dur   5 p
"By the Waters of the Minnetonka"—Lieurence
   Pres   1942   6 p
"Liebestraum"—Liszt-Black
   Bl   1942   3 p
"La Mandolinata"—Loukine
   Int   1914   2 p
"Wedding March" from "Midsummer Night's Dream"—
   Mendelssohn-Salzedo
   E-V   1942   2 p
"Nun's Prayer"—Oberthur
   Scho   4 p
"Souvenir de Lucia di Lammermoor"—Oberthur
   Hof   8 p
"Estrellita"—Ponce-J. Vito
   Bel   1942   6 p
"Prayer" from "Othello"—Rossini-Suerth
   Int   1917   4 p
"Barcarolle"—A. Rubinstein-Hasselmans
   Ham   4 p
"Deep River"—Salzedo
   CF   1925   3 p
"Londonderry Air"—Salzedo
   E-V   1945   2 p
"Träumerei"—Schumann-Alberti
   CF   1914   3 p
"Capriccio Melodieux"—Snoer
   Gie   1901   4 p

SELECTED HARP SOLOS FOR SCHOOL ASSEMBLIES

"Minstrel's Adieu to his Native Land"—Thomas
    Ash   6 p
"By the Brook"—Torgerson
    Dit   1920   6 p
"Wedding March" (Bridal Chorus) from "Lohengrin"—
    Wagner-Salzedo
    E-V   1942   3 p
"Roses of Picardy"—Wood-Macquarrie
    Chap   1942   6 p

Grade IV

"Concert Walzer"—Alberstotter
    SN   10 p
"Petites Pantins"—Bernheim
    Sen   6 p
"La Source"—Blumenthal
    Ash   10 p
"Clair de Lune"—Debussy-Coeur
    JJ   1929   6 p
"Deuxième Arabesque"—Debussy-Renie
    Dur   1904   6 p
"Premier Arabesque"—Debussy-Renie
    Dur   1906   6 p
"Lucia di Lammermoor" Harp Solo—Donizetti-Zabel
    from "Album of Solo Pieces" edited by Annie Louise David
    —Vol. I
    Sch   1916   8 p
"Variations on the Londonderry Air"—Grandjany
    Mk   1941   4 p
"Aeolian Harp"—Hasselmans
    from "Album of Solo Pieces" edited by David—Vol. I
    Sch   1916   7 p
"Reverie"—Hasselmans
    Led   1891   5 p
"Ballade"—Ibert
    Led   1917   8 p
"En Barque le Soir"—Ibert
    Led   1917   7 p
"Lake Scene" from "Adirondacks Sketches"—Pinto
    Int   1915   8 p
"Impromptu"—J. Guy Ropartz
    Dur   1927   6 p

THE HARP

"My Heart at Thy Sweet Voice"—Saint-Saens-N. S. Miller
    Bel   6 p
"Lamentation"—Salzedo
    CF   1924   7 p
"Quietude"—Salzedo
    CF   1924   5 p
"Brise du Soir"—Sauvage
    RJ   1901   7 p
"Leggenda"—Sodero
    Int   1920   11 p
"Blue Danube Waltz"—Johann Strauss-Macquarrie
    Chap   9 p
"Pattuglia Spagnuola"—Tedeschi
    from "Album of Solo Pieces" edited by David—Vol. I
    Sch   1916   5 p
"Ernani"—Fantasia—Verdi-Cheshire
    Cra   9 p
"The Old Refrain"—J. Vito
    Bel   1942   6 p
"Scherzo"—J. Vito
    Bel   1942   10 p
"Marguerite au Rouet"—Zabel
    Bes   8 p

CHAPTER VI

Music for the Advanced Harpist

THIS CHAPTER is devoted to a brief listing of solo and ensemble works for the advanced harpist. The author has attempted to include both well-known works for the instrument and some lesser-known works of equal merit and interest.

As in the previous chapter, the name of the publisher, and the number of actual music pages of the composition, and (whenever possible) the date of publication, are included. This information appears directly under the title of the composition and name of the composer. The letter "S" following the number of pages indicates that the composition is for solo harp.

Again, no attempt has been made to list the complete repertoire for the advanced harpist. This list is only representative of the best that is available. The great difficulty in obtaining foreign published music for the harp is now somewhat alleviated. Several American publishing houses (M. Baron; Schirmer; N. Y. C.; Elkan-Vogel, Philadelphia; etc.) are now able to supply American harpists with solo and ensemble music from many of the European publishers. Current listings of available harp music—both solo and ensemble—may be obtained by writing to American music publishing houses listed in the previous chapter.

(Listed alphabetically by composers):

"Sapphic Dance"—Dramatic Dance No. 2, for dancer with harp
   accompaniment—Bantock
   B & H   1909   11 p
"Fantasy Sonata"—viola and harp—Bax
   Mur   1927   39 p (score)

[175]

"Quintet" for strings and harp—Bax
    Mur   1919   22 p (score)
Fantasiestück", op. 87—harp and piano—Bazelaire
    Dem   1912   24 p (score)
"Concerto for Harp and Orchestra"—Berezowsky
    With cadenza by Salzedo
    E-V   1947   42 p (harp and piano)
"Madame Noy" for soprano voice, flute, clarinet, bassoon, harp, viola and bass—Bliss
    Ches   1921   8 p (score)
"Greetings" for Women's chorus, two French horns and harp— Brahms (Op. 17, No. 3)
    Sch   8 p (score)
"I Hear a Harp" for Women's chorus, French horn and harp— Brahms (Op. 17, No. 1)
    Sch   4 p (score)
"Song from Ossian's Fingal" for Women's chorus, two French horns, and harp—Brahms (Op. 19, No. 4)
    Sch   12 p (score)
"Song from Shakespeare's Twelfth Night—Come Away Death" for Women's chorus, two French horns, and harp—Brahms (Op. 17, No. 2)
"Divertissement—A la Française"—Caplet
    Dur   1925   7 p   S
"Divertissement—A l'Espagnole"—Caplet
    Dur   1925   7 p   S
"Dances" for harp and strings—Debussy
    I. Danse Sacrée; II. Danse Profane
    Dur   1904   28 p (harp and piano)
"Sonata" for flute, viola and harp—Debussy
    Pastorale, Interlude, Finale
    Dur   1915   36 p (score)
"Spanish Dance No. I"—de Falla-Grandjany
    AMP   1913   9 p   S
"Old English Suite"—Farnaby
    From the Fitzwilliam Virginal Book, transcribed for flute, harp and cello
    R.B.&W.   1933   16 p (score)
"Impromptu"—Fauré
    Dur   1904   13 p   S
"Fantaisie"—Gallon
    Rou   1921   21 p   S

MUSIC FOR THE ADVANCED HARPIST

"Concerto for Harp and Orchestra"—Glière
  EMl'U   1940   45 p (harp part)
"La Danse des Sylphes"—Godefroid
  SSM   10 p   S
"Suite" for flute, violin and harp—Goossens
  Impromptu, Serenade, Divertissement
  Ches   1917   29 p (score)
"Children at Play"—Grandjany
  Dur   1929   10 p   S
"Dans la Forêt du Charme et l'Enchantement"—Grandjany
  Dur   1923   10 p   S
"Rhapsodie"—Grandjany
  Rou   1922   12 p   S
"Valse Melancolique" for flute and harp—Grandval
  G & T   10 p (score)
"Bachkiria—Fantasy" for flute and harp—Gretchaninoff
  Scho   1932   11 p (score)
"Un Jour d'Eté" for soprano, with accompaniment of cello and
  harp—Gretchaninoff (Op. 131, No. 1)
  Scho   1934   5 p (score)
"Concerto in B♭"—Handel-Grandjany
  For harp alone, with cadenza by Grandjany
  Dur   1923   16 p
"Sonata for Harp"—Hindemith
  Moderately fast, Lively, Very slow
  AMP   1939   13 p   S
"Sonatine" for flute and harp—Inghelbrecht
  Led   1920   23 p (score)
"Danse Lente" for flute and harp—Jongen
  Ches   1924   7 p (score)
"Trio for harp, flute and cello" Op. 22—Lajtha
  Roz   1937   35 p (score)
"Four Danses Medievales" for flute and harp—Lauber
  Zim   1928   23 p (score)
  1. Rigaudon 2. Mascarde 3. Pavanne 4. Gaillarde
"Malaguena"—Lecuona-Grandjany
  Mk   1934   7 p   S
"Petite Symphonie Concertante" for harp, harpsichord, piano,
  and two string orchestras—Martin
  UE   1947   15 p (harp part)

"Suite" for flute, harp and string quartet—Mason
   Sarabande, Elegy, Caprice
   Sch   1923   31 p (score)
"Harping on a Harp"—Maxwell
   AAM   1947   3 p   S
"Suite—From Childhood" for harp and orchestra—McDonald
   E-V   1941   19 p (harp part)
"Concerto for flute, harp and orchestra"—Mozart
   H & R   1878   16 p (harp part)
"Cadenzas to Mozart Concerto"—for flute and harp alone
   B & H   8 p   Reinecke
   H & R   13 p   Thomas
"Concertino" for harp and orchestra—Oberthur
   Hof   31 p (harp and piano)
"Conte de Fées"—Oberthur
   Cos   1885   11 p   S
"Grand Concerto in G Minor" for harp and orchestra—Parish-
   Alvars
   H & R   39 p (harp part)
"Mosaique Musicale"—Parish-Alvars
   Scho   21 p   S
"Sonata Ia—Cinque Sonata Popolaresche Italiane"—Perrachio
   Car   1928   17 p   S
"Impromptu-Caprice"—Pierné
   Led   8 p   S
"Fantasie in Ges dur" for two harps—Poenitz
   Gie   1902   13 p (each harp part)
"Introduction and Allegro" for harp, flute, clarinet and string
   ensemble—Ravel
   Dur   1906   13 p (harp part)
"Pavane"—Ravel-Maganini
   Transcribed for harp and various combinations of instru-
   ments: flute and harp; violin, cello and harp; string quartet
   and harp; etc. Harp part edited by Lawrence.
   EM   1942   6 p (score)
"Concerto in C minor" for harp and orchestra—Renie
   G & T   64 p (harp and piano)
"Dance Caprice" for harp and piano (orchestra)—Renie
   Rou   19 p (score)
"Danse des Lutins"—Renie
   G & T   1912   10 p   S

The "Mozart Concerto in C Major" for flute and harp—first page of the score.
From the original publication by Breitkopf & Härtel, Leipzig—Ausgegeben 1881.
This work has recently been republished by Hargail Music Press, N.Y.C.

PLATE XXVII

[179]

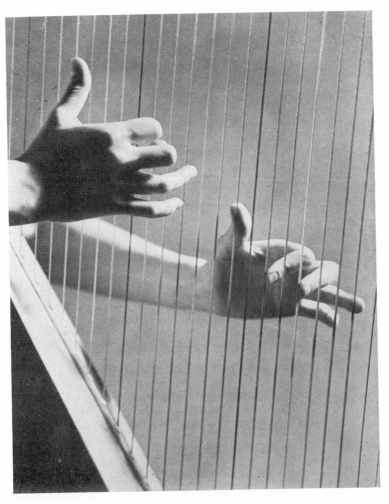

Hands on the harp strings. Posed by the author.

Photograph by Julie Rowe.

PLATE XXVIII

MUSIC FOR THE ADVANCED HARPIST

"Elegie" for harp and piano (orchestra)—Renie
    Rou   11 p (score)
"Legende d'Apres les Elfes de Leconte de Lisle"—Renie
    G & T   17 p   S
"Piece Symphonique"—Renie
    Rou   1913   12 p   S
    En trois episodes
"Ballade"—Salzedo
    Led   1913   15 p   S
"Sonata" for harp and piano—Salzedo
    Sch   1924   37 p (harp and piano)
"Poème—'Le Pavillon sur l'eau' d'après Theophile Gautier" for
    violin, viola, cello, flute and harp—Spelman
    Ches   1925   38 p (score)
"Rondo" for flute and harp—Spelman
    Ches   1929   19 p (score)
"Féerie, Prelude and Dance"—Tournier
    Rou   1912   16 p   S or for harp and string quartet
"Jazz-band"—Tournier
    Lem   1926   6 p   S
"Vers la Source dans le Bois"—Tournier
    Led   1922   8 p   S
"Choral et Variations" for harp and orchestra—Widor
    Heu   1900   19 p (harp part)
"Concerto in C Minor" for harp and orchestra—Zabel
    Zim   1904   29 p (harp part)
"La Source"—Zabel
    Bes   12 p   S

ADDITIONAL BIBLIOGRAPHY

GENERAL INFORMATION

A GENERAL HISTORY OF MUSIC—Charles Burney
(with critical and historical notes by Frank Mercer)
New York.   Harcourt, Brace & Co.   1935
In two volumes
See index for numerous references to the harp.

BOWED-HARP—Otto Andersen
London.   Reeves   1930   313 p

EOLUS (Eolian Review)—Carlos Salzedo, editor
Magazine published by National Association of Harpists
1921-1930.

FROM HARP TO HARPSICHORD—Karl Freund
International Studio magazine   August 1922
Vol. 75, pages 373-393

THE HARP AS A SOLO INSTRUMENT AND IN THE ORCHESTRA
—Alfred Kastner
Proceedings of the Musical Association   1908-1909
London.   Novello & Co.   1909   pages 1-14

THE HARP GOES TO PUBLIC SCHOOL—Elizabeth Searle Lamb
"Etude" magazine.   March 1949.
Pages 154, 190

HARP MUSIC—Helena Stone Torgerson
Chicago.   Lyon & Healy.   1916.   127 Pages

HISTORY OF THE HARP—Thomas Aptommas
New York.   Published by the author 1859.   55 Pages.

THE ORCHESTRA—Ebenezer Prout
London.   Augener Ltd.   1897.
Volume I—Technique of the instruments.
The Harp.   Pages 73-86.

REVIVE THE HARP BY REGENERATING THE REPERTOIRE OF THE
HARPISTS—Carlos Salzedo
"Musical America".   April 28, 1917.   Page 127.

THE SUTTON HOO MUSICAL INSTRUMENT—notes of lecture
given by R.L.S. Bruce Mitford.
"British Archaeological News Letter".   April 1948.
No. I.   Pages 11-13.
London.   J. Smith & Son printer.

THE HARP

Victor Book of Concertos—Abraham Veinus.
New York.   Simon & Schuster.   1948.
Handel Concerto.   Page 181.
Mozart Concerto.   Page 245.

Ancient Harp

Manners and Customs of the Ancient Egyptians—Sir J.
Gardner Wilkinson.
(New edition, revised and corrected—Samuel Birch).
New York.   Dodd, Mead & Co.   1878.   Vol. I.
Music of the Most Ancient Nations—Carl Engel.
London.   Reeves.   (1864) 1929.
See Index for numerous references to tne harp.
Sumerian Harp of Ur—Canon Galpin.
"Music & Letters".   April 1929.
Vol. X, No. 2.   Pages 108-123.

Old English, Irish, Welsh and Highland Harps

Brian Boru's Harp—W. J. Fitzpatrick.
"Irish Monthly".   1924.   Vol. 52.   Pages 666-668.
Description of Two Fitzgerald Harps of 17th Century—
Lord William Fitzgerald
"County Kildare Archaeological Society Journal".   1915.
Vol. 8.   Pages 133-149.
The Harp—Brinley Richards.
"Y Cymmrador".   April 1877.
Vol. I.   Pages 97-106.
On the Antiquity and Primitive Form of Our National
Instrument The Harp—Charles Egan.
"Journal British Archaeological Association"   1851.
Vol. 6.   Pages 103-116.
The Welsh Harper—John Parry.
London.   D'Almaie & Co.   October 1, 1839.

Foreign Language Works

Apφa—Ivan Alexandrovich Polomarenko.
Soviet Russia.   1939.   310 Pages.
Arpa e Arpisti—Blanda Bagatti.
Piacenza.   Societa Tip. Editoriale Porta.   1932.
82 Pages.

THE HARP

L'Arpa e il Suo Meccanismo—Maria Vittoria Grossi.
Bologna. Liberia Editrice Internazionale.
Luigi Beltrami. 1911. 22 Pages.

Die Harfe als Orchesterinstrument—Johannes Snoer.
Leipzig. C. Merseberger. 1898. 84 Pages.

Ein wort an die Herren Komponisten uber die praktische
verwendung der harfe in orchester, und verb. auff.
—Albert Zabel.
Leipzig. Zimmermann. 1899. 48 Pages.

Etudes des qualities artistiques et pratiques de la harpe
Pleyel "chromatique sans pedales"—Jean Risler.
Paris. Leduc. 1908. 88 Pages.

La Harpe et Ses Ancestres—Louis Schneider.
"La Nouvelle Revue". July-August 1903.
Pages 39-60.

La Harpe Moderne—Louis Laloy.
"La Revue Musicale". November 1902.
No. II (11). Pages 462-467.

BIOGRAPHICAL REFERENCES

American History and Encyclopedia of Music—
Editor W. C. Hubbard.
1908.

Baker's Biographical Dictionary of Musicians—Alfred Remy.
1919 (third edition).

Complete Encyclopedia of Music—John W. Moore.
1852.

Composers in America—Claire Reis.
1947 (revised and enlarged).

Cyclopedia of Music and Musicians—Oscar Thompson.
1939.

Oxford Companion to Music—Percy Scholes.
1945 (2nd American Edition).

United States Historical Records Survey, Wash., D. C.
1941.

"Hushed is the harp—the Minstrel gone."

SCOTT, *Lay of the Last Minstrel*

Index

An asterisk (*) following a page number indicates that the preceding name appears in Section III, Chapter IV. Further information can be obtained by consulting this listing.

INDEX

INDEX

[193]

THE HARP

INDEX

Ormandy, Eugene—55, 56, 57, 58, 59, 140
Ormandy, Stephanie (Steffy) Goldner —67, 72
Ossetes harp—63 (Plate XVII, 3)
Ostrowska, Djina—67
Oubradous, Fernand—134

Palestrina—142*
Palmgren, Selim—142*
Pampari, Graziella—67, 72
Pape, Henry—61
Paradisi, Pietro Domenico—142*
Paret, Betty—143*
Paris Conservatoire—48
Paris Conservatory Orchestra—56, 58
Paris Philharmonic Orchestra—145
Parish-Alvars, Elias—47, 48, 49, 50-51, 143*
Parker, Frances Jackson—73
Parkhurst, Howard E.—143*
Parry, John—143*
Parry, John Orlando—143*
Parts of the harp identified—86 (Plate XX)
Pasdeloup Orchestra—143
Pavese, Carlo—67
Peabody Conservatory of Music—72
Pedal harp—29, 35-39
Pergolesi, Giovanni B.—143*
Perrachio, Luigi—143*
Pescetti, Giovanni Battista—143*
Pessard, Emile L. F.—143*
Petrini, François—143*
Philadelphia Conservatory of Music—72
Philadelphia Musical Academy—72
Philadelphia Orchestra—55, 56, 57, 58, 59, 70, 130, 140
Phillips (Rosen), Edna—70, 72, 143*
Phonograph Recordings
1. Conductors—see name of individual conductor in Index.
2. Orchestral Works—see Section I, Chapter VI, pages 55-59.
3. Recording Musicians—
   a. Ensembles:
      Aeolians—123*
      Calvet Quartet—144
      Eddy Brown Ensemble—140
      Florentine Quartet—132*
      Gondolier Trio—143*
      Griller String Quartet—125

Neapolitan Trio—142*
"New Friends of Rhythm"—142
Paris Instrumental Quintet—131
Riveria Trio—145*
Stuyvesant Quartet—144
Trio de Luce—141, 150*
Venetian Trio—151*
Victor Chamber Orchestra—135, 144
Victor String Orchestra—130
Virtuoso String Quartet—144
   b. Harpists: See Section III, Chapter IV, pages 123-153.
      Names of recording harpists are given in full. Classical music recordings are listed under name of composer; popular music recordings are listed under name of harpist.
   c. Instrumentalists other than harpists:
      Barrere, flute—130, 144, 145
      Britt, cello—130, 144, 145
      Crunelle, flute—141
      Delecluse, clarinet—144
      Dinsey, violin—144
      Draper, clarinet—144
      Forbes, viola—125
      Ginto, viola—130
      Goossens, oboe—125
      Hilsberg, violin—152
      Hughes, piano—148
      James, cello—144
      Katims, viola—130
      Lemmone, flute—141
      LeRoy, flute—137
      Liebert, organ—141, 151
      Manouvrier, flute—126
      Mayes, cello—152
      McLane, clarinet—144
      Merckel, viola—130
      Mora, viola—130
      Morehouse, drums—150
      Moyse, flute—126, 130, 141
      Murchie, flute—144
      Primrose, viola—148
      Roens, viola—152
      Rose, cello—142
      Rudens, violin—152
      Ruderman, flute—125
      Slater, bass—125

[195]

INDEX